THE BIRTH FROM ON HIGH

Fr Matthew the Poor
&
Fr Athanasius Al-Maqary

THE BIRTH FROM ON HIGH

REFLECTIONS ON THE SPIRITUALITY AND HISTORY OF BAPTISM FROM THE MONASTERY OF ST. MACARIUS

Translated and Edited, with an Introduction by

Ramez Mikhail, PhD

Foreword by

Joseph Faltas, PhD

AGORA UNIVERSITY PRESS
2020

COPYRIGHT © 2020

AGORA UNIVERSITY PRESS

press.agora.edu

ALL RIGHTS RESERVED

No part of this publication may be reproduced, stored in a retrieval system, or transmitted in any form or by any means-electronic, mechanical, graphic, photocopy, recording, taping, information storage, or any other-without written permission of the publisher.

ISBN-13: 978-0-9848918-1-8

HIS HOLINESS **POPE TAWADROS II**
118th *Pope and Patriarch of the great city of Alexandria and the See of St. Mark.*

HIS HOLINESS **PATRIARCH IGNATIUS APHREM II KARIM**
Patriarch of Antioch and All the East.

PRINTED IN THE UNITED STATES OF AMERICA

Table of Contents

Foreword vii
Acknowledgment ix
Abbreviations xi
Prologue 1

Part I: Meditations on Baptism
Fr Matthew the Poor

The Baptismal Liturgy of Serapion of Thmuis 15
The Baptism of Christ 33
From the Jordan to Golgotha 39
The Holy Spirit & Christ's Death & Resurrection 47
Baptism and Unity with the Body of Christ 53
Baptism and Faith 59
With the Holy Spirit & Fire: The Birth of a Church 63

Part II: Baptism in History and the Fathers
Fr Athanasius Al-Maqary

Symbols and Types 73
Baptism & the Holy Spirit: Types from Scripture 79
The Time of Baptism 93
The Catechumenate 101
Infant Baptism 109
The Absolution of Women 123
Epilogue 137
Bibliography 139

Foreword

The fathers of the Church, including St Athanasius the Apostolic, drew a parallel between the creation of the first man, and his re-generation and renewal through the incarnation of the Word of God. This was the central idea of Athanasius' *On the Incarnation of the Word of God*. The fathers even meditated on the elements of creation, such as water, as the oldest of symbols mentioned in the first creation, and how the Spirit "was hovering" on the face of the water, to make of it a source of life, just as a bird lays over the eggs until they hatch and bring forth small chicks (the verb carries this meaning as well). The fathers also spoke about the element of water, and how the Holy Spirit "hovers" over it when it is sanctified by the prayer on the baptismal font until a living new creature comes forth from the Church's womb. This new creature is fed and nourished first of all by the true body and precious blood of the incarnate God, who desired in his love for man to grant us who believe in him to partake in Divine life, the life of the Trinity, granting us thereby to become sons of God, His heavenly Father, and temples of his Holy Spirit the Comforter.

In total awareness, the rites of the Coptic church express this strong connection between the mysteries of baptism and the Eucharist, and arranged for them to be accomplished together. This is not only done in a sequence unseparated in time and place, a fact with clear theological depth, but also in such a liturgical cohesiveness that reveals before us the depth of the mystery of the Divine dispensation and God's exceptional love, "who according to His abundant mercy has begotten us again to a living hope through the resurrection of Jesus Christ from the dead." (I Pet 1:3)

This cohesiveness and this connection are made clear with utmost clarity in the texts of the prayers of baptism and the Eucharist. Those who are to be baptized hear these supplications from the mouth of the priest, "May Christ take form in them that are to receive the baptism of the new birth...transform them, change them, sanctify them," and then hears the echo of these same actions together with the other members of the one body of Christ, the Church, after having been planted in the new olive tree. It is the same change that occurs on the bread and wine. The change in baptism then is none other than a change from a lower being to a new being, a being born from water and the Spirit, a being born, "not of the will of man, nor of the will of the flesh, but from God," (Jn 1:13) a being born from on high unto the inheritance of eternal life and incorruptibility. This being is now at that moment fed and nourished not with bread and wine for they have been sanctified and changed to become honored body and blood.

Among the gifts of the Divine incarnation, is that when the Son and Word of God came and renewed human nature, granting man the gift of the second birth, He also renewed the human senses, inflamed our awareness, and planted new energies for meditation, and in sum, "blessed our nature in Him." (Coptic Anaphora of St. Gregory the Theologian) Thus, these gifts became an inheritance to everyone who loves and sacrifices, in imitation of Him in whose image and likeness we were created, and in obedience to His commandments.

This book presents to us bright meditations and spiritual and deeply ascetic riches, derived from the living tradition of the Church and the writings of the fathers. These are the meditations of men who loved and sacrificed much, and thus came to understand that the mysteries deliver to us Christ Himself through the Holy Spirit. This is communicated in prayers that reflect a return of consciousness and encourage attention in us as worshippers in order to enter into the depth of that which exists before us, and partake of Him and live thereby, and thus rejoice and glorify His name for He was merciful to us and gave birth to us from on high, and thus we were made into citizens of heaven, and members of the household of God.

Joseph Moris Faltas, PhD
Washington, DC
Theophany, 2013

Acknowledgment

This volume is intended to fill a lack in understanding the theology of baptism in the Orthodox Church, as well as how the Coptic rite of baptism reflects and embodies this theology. As part of my theological studies in the University of Balamand and the St Stephen Course in Orthodox Theology, I became quickly aware of the general lack of availability of well written, easily accessible works on the theology and rites of baptism in the Coptic Church. A student of liturgical theology such as I, or indeed anyone wanting to learn about the Orthodox theology of baptism, can indeed gain valuable knowledge from Chrysostom's *Baptismal Instructions*, the *Catechetical Lectures* of Cyril of Jerusalem, or Ambrose' *On the Mysteries*. More recently, Fr Alexander Schmemann's *Of Water and the Spirit* is also a masterpiece, capable of imparting much in the way of theological depth and traditional yet fresh treatment of a number of critical modern-day issues based on the baptismal rite of the Orthodox Church. As indispensable as these works and many others are, a gap exists between works written based on the baptismal rite of the Eastern Orthodox tradition, and those written, primarily in Arabic, and are based on the baptismal rite of other Orthodox families, such as the Coptic Church. This book fills this gap by providing those interested in the Orthodox liturgical theology of baptism as it is embodied in the Coptic baptismal rite with an in-depth treatment based on the common, mutual tradition of Orthodox patristic heritage.

The translation presented here comes from two different sources. Part One of this work, Meditations on Baptism, is a translation of some of the writings of Fr Matthew the Poor (*Matta Al-Maskin*), one of the most famous and well respected figures in contemporary Egyptian monasticism. The late Fr Matthew was a prolific author, and a sophisticated thinker and theologian, having dedicated his life to studying the Scriptures and the writings of the fathers. The chapters selected here for translation come from a rather large work by Fr Matthew titled *Baptism: The First Origins of Christianity*. Part Two, Baptism in History and the Fathers, is a translation of three chapters that appeared in a book titled *The Baptism of Water and the Spirit* by Fr

Athanasius Al-Maqary, a monk in the monastery of St Macarius in the Nitria desert in Egypt. Fr Athanasius is a prolific author and liturgical theologian, who has written a large number of works in the last decade on the theology and rites of the different sacraments, as well as various seasons of the Coptic Church.

I thank God first and foremost for allowing me the opportunity, the time, and the discipline to produce this translation in this quality. I pray that God has allowed this work to come to fruition in order to be a source of edification and benefit for those who read it, for the glory of his Church. In addition, many people have participated in the production of this book, and it is a pleasure for me to thank them by name. First, I wish to thank Fr Bishoy Mikhail Brownfield, my spiritual father, without whom I would not have been introduced to the great figure of Fr Matthew the Poor, or embarked on this edifying journey of studying the rites of the Church. I also wish to thank Fr Daniel Habib, the pastor of St John Coptic Orthodox parish in Covina, CA. Fr Daniel was the first to encourage me in selecting these two texts as a potential academic project in the St Stephen Course in Orthodox Theology. His enthusiasm and encouragement helped push me forward and gain the determination to realize this project.

The inestimable help of my brother in Christ, Emmanuel Gergis, need not go unmentioned. Emmanuel's vision and creativity were of great help in selecting the chapters for translation and charting the scope and objective of this volume. I thank God for his unwavering dedication to the theological life of the Church, and I look forward to many years of teamwork and cooperation with him for the glory of God. I am also indebted to the invaluable help of my beloved wife Marianne, who spent many nights proofreading the translation and offering various stylistic suggestions. More importantly, her constant support of my studies and various projects shows a great deal of love, patience, and sacrifice. Last but not least, I wish to thank the Saint Cyril Orthodox Christian Society for making this translation available, and for generally encouraging academic and educational work in Orthodox Theology. May everyone be rewarded for their help and support.

Ramez Mikhail
Theophany, 2012

Abbreviations

ACW	Ancient Christian Writers Series
ANF	Ante-Nicene Fathers Series
DACL	*Dictionnaire d'Archéologie Chrétienne et de Liturgie*
NPNF-I	Nicene and Post-Nicene Fathers, Series I
NPNF-II	Nicene and Post-Nicene Fathers, Series II
ODCC	*The Oxford Dictionary of the Christian Church*
PG	Patrologia Graeca
PO	Patrologia Orientalis

Prologue

Baptism as an Ecclesial Event

Within the first few pages of Fr Alexander Schmemann's classic work on Baptism, *Of Water and the Spirit*, one is immediately made aware of the current crisis of baptism in popular piety. Fr Alexander quickly brings our attention to the ignorance of most Christians today of the paschal tone of baptism, and that baptism itself has become absent from the Church's *leitourgia*, her piety, and our entire worldview.[1] This crisis is blamed mainly on scholastic Western influence on Orthodox theology, which for centuries has severed baptism from its connection to the rest of the *ecclesia*, a connection that is actualized in the Eucharist. Indeed, the question whether baptism is ecclesial and connected to the Eucharist is in itself evidence that this is a real crisis. For this would not have been a question in need of an answer if, in the words of Fr Alexander, "our modern dogmatical and canonical consciousness... [were not] ignorant of the old principle *lex orandi lex est credendi*."[2]

The short answer, therefore, is that baptism is ecclesial *because* it is actualized, fulfilled, and crowned, in the Eucharist, "the sacrament of the Church."[3] One therefore cannot speak of an *ecclesial* baptism without speaking of a *Eucharistic* baptism, and vice versa. Unfortunately, what the so-called "Western pseudomorphosis"[4] of the Eastern Church (whether Chalcedonian or non-Chalcedonian), spoken against by Fr Alexander, has done is compartmentalize the sacraments, and privatize the religious experience. In other words, under this influence, baptism became a self-sufficient sacrament, disconnected from any other liturgical act, and concerns only the person being baptized, the exact opposite of ecclesial and Eucharistic. Taken

---

[1] *Of Water and the Spirit* (Crestwood, NY: St. Vladimir Seminary Press, 1995), 8
[2] Ibid., 10
[3] Ibid., 117
[4] Ibid. Cf. other works by Fr Alexander Schmemann, where the theme of Western pseudomorphosis and the negative influence of Scholasticism on the sacraments occur frequently.

to an extreme, the West has long ago severed baptism from Chrismation and the Eucharist. However, even in traditions where baptism and the Eucharist are still connected by canonical force, as in the Coptic tradition as one example of many, this separation between baptism, the *ecclesia*, and the Eucharist can still be seen, visible every time a baptism is performed, where the Eucharist takes a backseat in the people's piety, satisfied merely as a canonical requirement, and offering an occasion for a few photographs of the infant's first communion.

In this limited space, therefore, I will attempt to support Fr Alexander's thoughts concerning the ecclesial and Eucharistic aspects of Baptism. For this end, this treatment will go beyond merely repeating what Fr Alexander has so beautifully expressed, though at times doing so will be indispensable. Rather, I will add historical and theological evidence as necessary, in support of the strong link between baptism, the *ecclesia*, and the sacrament that unites it all, the Eucharist.

Perhaps one of the strongest indications of the ecclesial character of baptism comes from St Paul's first epistle to the Corinthians, to whom he says, "For by one Spirit we were all baptized into one body—whether Jews or Greeks, whether slaves or free—and have all been made to drink into one Spirit." (I Cor 12:13) By its very nature, baptism is our initiation into the one body of Christ. As such, it necessitates the participation and assistance of the entire body for this process of initiation to be truly effective and made real. It is not surprising that Fr Alexander quickly laments how "Baptism today has become a private family celebration performed as a rule outside the corporate worship of the Church."[5] Unfortunately, baptism seems to have lost this ecclesial character at some point in Christian history – whether because of Western influence or other factors is beyond the scope of this writing – though it is clearly at the very core of the biblical spirit of baptism. Perhaps part of the reason is that we no longer understand the role of the Church community in the initiation of neophytes?

Fr Alexander relates to us the role of the community in infant baptism in such a profound way that should help us understand part of the ecclesial character of baptism in general. Of course, the com-

---

[5] Ibid., 8

mon objection to infant baptism is that infants are too young to possess any real faith in Christ or understanding of the sacrament they are about to receive. To this, Fr Alexander responds by distancing Orthodoxy itself from the debate over infant baptism, because the Church "never accepted the reduction of faith to 'personal faith' alone, which made that debate inevitable."[6] Rather, it is the faith of Christ – found in and handed down by the Church – that truly converts the soul and fulfills baptism. Whether we are speaking about infant or adult baptism, we must remember that no one's faith is enough to make this conversion, this death and Resurrection with Christ, complete and whole. In fact, "It is on the faith of the Church that baptism depends; it is the faith of the Church that makes baptism that which it is."[7] Since the Church is nothing but the body of Christ, the community of believers, we can therefore see the strong ecclesial character of baptism, that which is indispensable to its function and role as integration into the one body of Christ. Whether infant or adult, the faith and role of the Church herself cannot be ignored.

Historical accounts of baptism in the Church's early centuries show clearly baptism's strong ecclesial character. As early as the 2nd century AD. we see in the *Didache* evidence of the community's involvement in the baptism of adults. Instructing how baptisms are to be performed, the author of the *Didache* writes, "But before the baptism, let the baptizer fast, and the baptized, *and whatever others can.*"[8] Not only was the baptized and the priest or bishop celebrating the baptism required to fast, but anyone in the community who was able to do so. A similar reference to a community fast, which very likely was the precursor of Lent, occurs in the mid-second century in the *First Apology* of Justin Martyr: "They [the catechumens] are instructed to pray and to entreat God with fasting, for the remission of their sins that are past, we praying and fasting with them."[9]

In a more detailed account of the level of community involvement in the reception of catechumens, the *Apostolic Tradition* relates how those advancing to the catechumenate are to be scrutinized for the sincerity of their intentions, relying heavily on the community's

---

[6] Ibid., 67
[7] Ibid., 69
[8] *Didache* VII (ANF 7:379), emphasis added.
[9] Justin Martyr *First Apology* LXI (ANF 1:183)

knowledge and trust of them: "Those who brought them [the catechumens] shall bear witness whether they have the ability to hear the word. They might be questioned about their state of life, whether he has a wife, or whether he is a slave."[10] The faith entrusted to the Church community is truly the precious possession of the people of God. Since baptism depends on this ecclesial faith, we see here this understanding embodied in the community holding itself responsible for inquiring about those wanting to join. A similarly detailed account comes to us from the travels of Egeria the Spanish pilgrim (4th century). In her description of the reception of catechumens in Jerusalem, she describes a similar scene of assembly and inquiry, "As they [the catechumens] come in one by one, the bishop asks their neighbors questions about them: 'Is this person leading a good life? Does he respect his parents? Is he a drunkard or a boaster?' He asks about all the serious human vices."[11] Such a strong emphasis on community responsibility testifies to the ecclesial character of baptism in a way that is truly absent from our modern baptisms.

A glimpse of this ecclesial character can be seen in the prayers of the baptismal service itself. One of the earliest extant baptismal texts available to us, that of Serapion of Thmuis (ca. 4th century) contains a *Prayer for the Anointing of the Catechumens*, in which the priest prays, "Let them be gathered and reunited to the flock of the Lord and of our Savior Jesus Christ. Let them share with the saints the promised inheritance."[12]

The current Byzantine rite of baptism also reflects this ecclesial character from the very start, where the priest is instructed to put on white garments before the service. Commenting on this rubric, Fr Schmemann clarifies that this is a clear indication of the joyful, paschal character of baptism, which necessarily implies the participation of the entire people of God, acknowledging its own passage from this world to the kingdom.[13] Similarly, in the Coptic rite the priest prays *A Prayer of the Laying-on of Hands on the Catechumens*, in which there is a

---

[10] *On the Apostolic Tradition* (Crestwood, NY: St. Vladimir Seminary Press, 2001), 98
[11] John Wilkinson *Egeria's Travels* (Oxford, 1999), 162
[12] Lucien Deiss *Springtime of the Liturgy* (Collegeville, MN: The Liturgical Press, 1979), 202
[13] Schmemann, 38

petition to "make them sheep of the holy flock of your Christ, purified members of the catholic Church,"[14] a clear reminder that baptism, aside from being simply an abolishing of the consequences of ancestral sin, is more profoundly an initiation into the *ecclesia*, the flock of Christ. How difficult it is then to justify a private event designed primarily to integrate us into a community? This is especially clear when we take into account the Eucharistic aim and goal of baptism.

Since the Eucharist is truly "the sacrament of the Church"[15] it follows that baptism, the initiation into the Church, is necessarily an initiation into the Eucharist first and foremost. If baptism is death and Resurrection with Christ enabling us to receive our personal Pentecost in Chrismation, then by comparison, our birth and reception of the Holy Spirit in these sacraments allow us to enter the Church, to become members of the one body of Christ. This process of integration into the Church following baptism and chrismation is revealed most clearly in the procession from the baptistery to the Church, especially in the original rite of baptism.

Traditionally, when Lent was the Church's catechetical season and baptisms were performed in the Paschal vigil, the Paschal procession was itself the baptismal procession.[16] Those who were baptized were led in procession to the closed church doors, the original royal doors, where the congregation waited. Together, they all entered the Church proclaiming, "Christ is risen!" This beautiful ritual embodied a clear link between baptism and entering the Church, becoming a member of the Church, and living the Lord's Pascha as the Pascha of the baptized and the entire Church. Fr Schmemann sums this up, pointing that "Baptism fulfills itself as *procession* to the Church into the Eucharist: the participation in Christ's Pascha 'at his table, in his kingdom' (Lk 22:15-16)."[17]

Perhaps on a more fundamental level, baptism can be said to be Eucharistic insofar as man himself is ontologically a Eucharistic being. After all, thanksgiving is man's true and original vocation. It is, in the words of Fr Schmemann, "the state of perfect man…the life

---

[14] Coptic Orthodox Diocese of the Southern United States, *The Holy Baptism* (Colleyville, TX: 2010), 162
[15] Schmemann, 117
[16] Cf. Josef Jungmann, *The Early Liturgy to the Time of Gregory the Great* (London: Darton, Longman & Todd, 1959), 79
[17] Schmemann, 113

of paradise."[18] Born in the image and likeness of God, man's cosmic role as priest was to bring God's creation back to God in thanksgiving and adoration, the only true response to God's creation and gifts. By doing so, man fulfills the meaning of the prayer "We offer unto You these gifts from what is Yours."[19] Therefore, insofar as baptism can be said to be a restoration of man to his original state, his original priestly role so to speak, baptism itself can be said to be Eucharistic, a re-creation of man as the Eucharistic being he was meant to be.

We can summarize therefore and say that the ecclesial character of baptism, as well as its connection to the Eucharist, is one and the same thing. The unanimous witness of the Church fathers and early Church documents testify to the strong ecclesial nature of baptism in the first centuries. Not only was baptism an annual major event, but also the community at large was involved in the acceptance of catechumens, was often asked about the sincerity of their conversion, and was encouraged to fast with them in preparation. The intersection between baptism, Church, and Eucharist is most apparent in the baptismal-Paschal procession, where the *ecclesia* meets the baptized, and together they enter into the Eucharist, the sacrament of the kingdom. In many ways, the selections chosen for this book examine in greater detail the themes discussed above. Below is a short outline and commentary on the selected texts.

The Text

A word must be said regarding the style of the works translated. Neither of the two fathers whose works are presented here received formal theological training in the Western academic sense. Both Fr Athanasius and Fr Matthew have led – and in the case of Fr Athanasius, continue to lead – outstandingly ascetic lives in the deserts of Egypt for most of their lives. The thoughts, reflections, and ideas presented here are the result of their independent scholarly efforts, and more importantly, their own personal life of contemplation in Jesus Christ. As such, a reader who is used to reading Western academic works,

---

[18] *For the Life of the World: Sacraments and Orthodoxy* (Crestwood, NY: St. Vladimir Seminary Press, 1973), 37
[19] The Divine Liturgy of St. Basil the Great in the Coptic tradition.

written in a certain recognizable style of argumentation, validation, and flow of discourse, might find here something quite different. That is why the selections chosen are presented as *reflections*, to emphasize the less academic nature of the authors' writing, though as the reader will quickly realize, the academic rigor is not at all lacking. Nonetheless, one should not be quick to misjudge these works as unsophisticated or lacking in depth. On the contrary, as the unfolding pages will reveal, our authors make full use of all the early patristic and modern sources on the subject that would be expected of any academic work of the highest caliber. More importantly, I have found that there is much to be learned from the humility of the desert; a certain simplicity, clarity, and straightforwardness that cannot be paralleled in many of today's academically sophisticated theological writings. One can immediately grasp this humility and straightforwardness in Fr Matthew's own introduction to his work, where he writes,

> Before anything else, I admit that I am not a specialist in rituals, especially the rite of baptism, nor did I ever baptize anyone in my life. But those who have read my book on the Eucharist pleaded that I write a book on baptism on the same level, which frightened me and I refused for years, convinced that I am unqualified to write about baptism...
>
> However, out of a strong jealousy over the heritage of the Church, which has started to be increasingly forgotten, I could not restrain myself. I cried and wept in front of God to grant me in my old age this gift, to be able to document and preserve the Church's tradition.

With such insight in mind, I would like to make a few comments regarding the sources used in the following pages, particularly in Part Two, Baptism in History and the Fathers. Many times, Fr Athanasius relies on Arabic translations of key sources. Some of these Arabic translations are readily available in English translations. Such works include patristic sources available in the Nicene and Post-Nicene Fathers series, Ancient Christian Writers series, and others. In cases where the text was readily available in English, the English translation was used, instead of translating Fr Athanasius' Arabic text. Other times, no readily accessible English translation was available. In some such cases, the passage was translated directly from the original language. One particular case appears in Chapter 2, where a passage is cited from Didymus' *De Trinitate*, of which, to my knowledge, no English translation is available. The Greek text was supplied in the footnote. In other cases, Fr Athanasius' Arabic text was translated verbatim, and a footnote was added indicating this.

In very few cases, Fr Athanasius' citation was either entirely lacking or was clearly erroneous. Sometimes, the work cited has little to do with the information at hand, while other times, the citation fails to indicate any specific edition or publication information for the work cited, making it very difficult – if not impossible – to verify the information. Finally, some citations were copied wholesale from another source that contains them, and those oftentimes were lacking in information as well. In all these cases, the utmost effort was spent in tracing and verifying all the information. When all attempts failed, an editorial footnote was added, showing such problems. Nonetheless, it is my hope that such infrequent problems will not detract from the overall value of this work. Finally, regarding Scriptural citations, all verses were used from the NKJV, and using NKJV numbering.

PART ONE

Meditations on Baptism

Fr Matthew the Poor

1

The Baptismal Liturgy of Serapion of Thmuis

In the early Church, the sacrament of baptism was a highly solemn and dignified event. There were many prayers associated with the baptism rite that explained the importance of baptism, and pointed the attention of both the baptized and their families to the significance of the sacrament.

One of the oldest baptismal texts was written ca. AD 350 and attributed to Serapion of Thmuis. This saintly figure is very prominent in the liturgical history of the Coptic Church, and is sometimes given the title Scholasticus for his erudition. Serapion is also the author of the famous *Euchologion of Serapion of Thmuis*, and contributed to establishing the prayers of baptism and the Eucharistic liturgy in the church at the time. He was also a contemporary and close friend of Athanasius, as well as a friend and monastic colleague of Antony the Great. From *The Life of Antony* written by Athanasius, we learn that Antony bequeathed one of his two sheepskin cloaks to him, while the other was given to Athanasius himself. The Coptic Church commemorates St Serapion on March 21st.[1]

Needless to say, while I recount the status and dignity of baptism in AD 350, I cannot help but feel saddened at the current lack of understanding and appreciation of it. However, my intention here is to awaken the reader's conscience to the importance of the Church's return to her glorious tradition and a deep knowledge of the Church's rites, sacraments, and theology.

The rite of baptism shows the relationship between baptism and the celebration of Pascha, which was highly celebrated by the whole Church with joy, singing, and a magnificent procession, the remnants

---

[1] This does not seem to be the case in the current *Coptic Synaxarium*.

of which still exist, albeit hardly understood in terms of its theological depth. This link between the two was felt intensely, such that once the annual administration of baptism approached, the people of the church also felt the immanent approach of Pascha.

Even more so, the reader will realize without any exaggeration that, through baptism, the Church is brought in touch with herself and her value as a mother, who gives birth to new children every year, and receives them with hymns and rituals, accompanied with the explanation of baptism itself to the baptized through the bishop's exhortations. The rite of baptism was a reviving of the liturgy of Pascha and the rituals of the Church as a mother. Unfortunately, the current absence of the baptism rite in all its fullness, because of its restriction to the baptism of infants, causes the Church to feel infertile, and robs her of this wonderful annual joy. In the following pages, we will offer some meditations on the baptismal prayers as they have come down to us in the *Euchologion of Serapion of Thmuis*.

The Consecration of the Baptismal Water

The first act in the baptismal rite is the consecration of the water. The priest stands in front of the baptismal font, dressed in the special white garments of baptism, and recites the following prayer:

> King and Lord of all things, Creator of the universe, through the Incarnation of Your Only-begotten Son, Jesus Christ, you have given to all created nature the grace of salvation; you redeemed your creation through the coming of your unutterable Word. Look down now from the height of heaven and cast your eyes on these waters. Fill them with the Holy Spirit. Let your unutterable Word be in them, let him transform their power. Let him give them the power to be fruitful, let him fill them with your grace, so that the mystery which is to be accomplished may bear fruit in those who will be regenerated and may fill with your Divine grace all those who go down (into the baptismal font) and are baptized. You who love men, be gracious, take pity on those you have

created, save your creation, the work of your right hand. Transfigure all those who are going to be reborn with your Divine and indescribable beauty. Transfigured and regenerated, let them thus be saved and 'judged worthy of your kingdom.' (2 Thess 1:5) Just as the Word, your Only-begotten Son, by descending into the waters of the Jordan bestowed sanctification upon them, so let him now descend into these waters to make them Holy and spiritual, so that the baptized may no longer be flesh and blood, but may become spiritual. Let them be able to adore you, the eternal Father, through Jesus Christ, in the Holy Spirit. Through him, glory to you and power, for ever and ever, Amen.[2]

The fact that baptism starts with the consecration of water has a very deep spiritual and theological meaning, which will be explained shortly. Sadly, today we find that many parishes, due to a lack of understanding of this spiritual and theological importance of consecrating the water, have decided not to "waste time", both theirs and the people's. Thus, they resorted to a radical reductionism of the rite, which wastes its meaning, as well as its power, value, and theology all at once. Instead of consecrating the water, they are satisfied with a small amount of pre-consecrated water poured into the new water without any prayers in order to please themselves and the people, who always demand the shortening of services. Even more, some parishes have completely eliminated the baptismal font, leaving the Church as a woman without a womb. All this is the result of ignorance of the holiness of this sacrament, its importance, and its value. More importantly, this is the result of a severing of the tradition of the early Church from the consciousness of the *contemporary Christian*. So reduced baptism has become, that in ten minutes or less a human being is made a Christian, a member of the body of Christ, a holy vessel to contain the Holy Spirit of God, and to put on Christ himself! In effect, all that is needed is a certificate of baptism. No wonder therefore that the baptismal rite has declined and become ridiculed in the minds of the people. It is not the rite alone that is thus virtually

---

[2]Deiss, 200.

ignored in their eyes, but the Church herself, which has lost her value, her necessity, through these seemingly unintelligible sacraments. As a result, the meaning of *the new man, the new creation, the new life*, or *the newness of life* was completely lost on the Christian person, rendering doctrine itself as burdensome and abstruse rhetoric.

The priest has failed to instruct the people that the consecration of the baptismal water is exactly like the consecration of bread and wine that is transformed into the spiritual food of Truth, which nourishes the spirit not the flesh. Similarly, through the same type of prayer —sanctification through thanksgiving – the baptismal water changes from its original dead nature to a living nature, birth giving, capable of bestowing the new and invisible spiritual life. This is the first process of sanctification that the Church performs through the power of Christ, who was baptized in the Jordan, transforming it into water for the new life, "For thus it is fitting for us to fulfill all righteousness." (Mt 3:15)

In fact, water is one of the oldest religious symbols and is responsible for the first creation, when before all creation the Spirit hovered over the surface of the water in the first chapter of Genesis. Thus, it was understood that the water and the Spirit were the sources of creation. At the same time, water became the symbol of death in the story of Noah and the ark, where we read about the depths that destroyed all of mankind, while only eight souls were saved. These souls were the family of Noah concerning which St Peter wrote, "There is also an antitype which now saves us—baptism (not the removal of the filth of the flesh, but the answer of a good conscience toward God), through the Resurrection of Jesus Christ." (1 Pet 3:21) In this manner, the depths of the water refer to the habitation of evil spirits and the threat of death, which appears frequently in the Psalms. Water was this unfathomable element, uncontrollable in the dark corners of the world. Just as water was the beginning of life, it was also the descent of death and destruction. Water was portrayed this way in the Old Testament.

Water was also an element of purification in the Scriptures. This is why Christ chose water to be the origin and principle of the washing away of sins, and of the new birth in his dialogue with Nicodemus. Nonetheless, this is not of the very nature of water, but only after its sanctification and the descent of the Spirit on it that "one is born of water and the Spirit." (Jn 3:5) Thus, the new life is bestowed by the

Holy Spirit and the water, whose nature has been transformed, being revealed now as a new nature, a new creation, capable of communion with God.

For just as water and the Spirit that hovered over it are considered the sources of the first material creation, likewise water and the Spirit that descends upon it through prayer are considered the sources of the second spiritual creation in the new world, which God loved, and for which he gave his only Son for its salvation. Thus, after its sanctification, water reflects the image of God through the new spiritual creation that proceeds from him.

Look therefore, dear reader, at the priest, standing before the baptismal font, consecrating the water, making it into a divine and heavenly womb for a new spiritual creation that resembles its creator in glory and holiness. Do not think this is incredible, but rather remember the descent of Christ into the Jordan to transform its water into the source of the new baptism! Water here became much more than water! Here, an entirely new nature has been revealed for the water of baptism, since Christ has transformed it into the basis of the new creation: "Go therefore and make disciples of all the nations, baptizing them in the name of the Father and of the Son and of the Holy Spirit." (Mt 28:19)

Contemplate with me this amazing paradoxical function of water: the source of the first material creation, and the source of divine wrath and collective annihilation, that is, the source of life and death. In this same pattern, the Church used water in the sacrament of baptism, making it, in the burial of the baptized under water three times, a symbol of the death of Christ and his burial, and in rising from the water, the symbol of rising with Christ unto a new life. The intention here is to strengthen and confirm the faith of the baptized in a very practical and real way. The baptized participates *really* and practically in the death and burial of Christ. Then, upon rising from the water, the baptized has been formed by the Holy Spirit in the likeness of the Resurrection of Christ from the tomb to a new life, as well as to signify his state of partaking in Christ's Resurrection. Thus, water becomes a medium of death and Resurrection with Christ. It is important to remember here that what transforms this act to a spiritual reality identical with the reality of faith is the Holy Spirit, one of whose functions is to "take of what is mine and declare it to you." (Jn

16:14) That is, the unknown works of Christ are made by the Holy Spirit completely known to us and in us.

Thus, we see that the prayer of consecration of the water gives it content and purpose. The content is the ability to give the new life by the life-giving Spirit, while the purpose is the grace of being able to enter the kingdom of God, the direct goal of the new life. In this way we see that whoever obtains this threefold immersion in water together with the threefold confession of the Holy Trinity immediately starts longing for and seeking after the kingdom of God. Next, the Church begins to teach this person how to reach the kingdom through grace, moral conduct, love, and simplicity of heart. For the grace that descends from God upon the baptized is that which sets his heart aflame with the love of the kingdom and the pursuit of it. Likewise, he hears this grace through the explanation of the gospel by the bishop and as a goal for this holy sacrament. This grace accompanies the baptized on his long journey towards a difficult yet desirable crossing, a mystical, invisible passage from this passing world to the world of the Spirit and the blessings of the age to come, and enlightens him in order to understand the reality of that which is passing, and that which abides forever.

We have now realized the value of consecrating the water, which prepares it to be, along with the Holy Spirit, a medium of the new birth, according to the description of Christ to Nicodemus. In a deeply spiritual way, the consecration liberates the water from its initial nature, which is dead, deadening, and suitable only for the habitation of evil spirits, to a new nature, alive and quickening, suitable for the dwelling of the Holy Spirit for the birth of the new man. In this way, water is prepared for the divine presence, in essence becoming the beginning of the transfiguration of matter in the world. The world itself begins to be re-created anew with the creation of the new man. Indeed, this new creation of man through baptism is expressed by John the evangelist as light, "in him was life, and the life was the light of men." (Jn 1:4) In other words, we proceed from the enlightenment of baptism, to the light of the Eucharist, where we enter into the full encounter of the risen Lord, in whom is our life.

Behold, dear reader, the importance of knowing all this theological depth of baptism! If we neglect this, will we not be unfaithful in what we received, what we inherited, and what we ought to live?

A Prayer for the Baptized

Serapion of Thmuis wrote:

> We pray you, O God of Truth, for your servant here. We ask you to make him worthy of the Divine mystery and your unutterable regeneration. For it is to you who love men that we offer him, it is to you that we consecrate him. According to your grace, let him share in this regeneration, let him no longer be under the influence of any baleful and wicked spirit; but let him serve you at all times, let him keep your commandments, let the Word, your Only-begotten Son, guide him. Through him, glory to you and power, in the Holy Spirit, now and for ever and ever! Amen.[3]
>
> You who love men, benefactor, Savior of all who turn to you: Be gracious to this servant of yours; let your right hand lead him to regeneration. Let your Only-begotten Son, the Word, bring him to the baptismal font. Let his new birth be honored, let your grace not be fruitless. Let your Holy Word be at his side, let your Holy Spirit be with him, let him repel and put to flight every temptation. Through your Only-begotten Son, Jesus Christ, glory to you and power, now and forever and ever. Amen.[4]
>
> God, O God of Truth, Creator of the universe and Lord of all creation, fill your servant here with your blessing. Make him share in the angelic powers, so that henceforth he who has had a part in your divine and profitable grace, may be no longer "flesh" but "spirit".[5] Keep him for yourself to the very end, O Creator of all things, Through your Only-begotten

---

[3] Ibid., 201
[4] Ibid., 203
[5] Cf. Jn 3:6

Son, Jesus Christ, glory to you and power, in the
Holy Spirit, now and forever and ever. Amen[6]

Let us meditate on these prayers. It is surprising indeed that some ignorant people still maintain that baptism is some sort of magic, which the clergy perform and call a mystery, as in something hidden from all except a select few, akin to pagan mystery cults. In fact, the Church is responsible for this in that she does not teach the people what is accomplished in baptism. These prayers have formed part of the Church's liturgical tradition since AD 350, yet the disappearance of such a beautiful tradition from the hearts and minds of the faithful is a great loss for the Church and the whole people.

In the prayers of sanctification and consecration of the water and the baptized, the bishop stands as a representative of the whole world, in the likeness of Adam himself the way he was meant to be, praying and entreating for the redemption of matter and man together. This matter, and man, Adam had caused to fall through his sin, and caused every man and the whole creation to inherit his fallen nature. The bishop therefore stands struggling in the name of Jesus Christ for a whole new creation, which Christ himself has brought into being with his baptism in the Jordan – when it was first proclaimed – and with the cross, the tomb, and the Resurrection – when it was finally proclaimed – as new elements, introduced into the world to renew it and re-create it.

When the bishop stands to offer these prayers and thanksgivings to God, he does so as a free creation, made free with Truth by Christ the True One. This having been accomplished, he is now free to intercede on behalf of whatever and whoever remains a slave to the world and Satan. Through his prayers, matter and the human being himself become free with Christ and in Christ, and water, as well as the person, rises to a superior nature directly connected to God in Christ and the Holy Spirit. It is as though the bishop takes us into paradise through his prayers as he sanctifies the water and the person, when the different natures are revealed according to their original states in their pure essence as created by God.

In these prayers, the bishop commemorates all the salvific acts of God, from his Incarnation and redemption to his Resurrection and

---

[6] Deiss, 203

the new eternal creation, created by his breath from water and the Spirit. These prayers have a pleasing efficacy in the eyes of God and Christ. They are a confession of God's grace, a thanksgiving, and a remembrance of his mercies and gifts through which he has restored man's nature, which has become corrupted, debased, has resisted God, and blasphemed against his name. Here the bishop recounts how God has proclaimed his mercy and restored his kingdom after man has refused his initial dignified life with him, having degenerated to sin and caused himself, and the entire creation with him, to fall under the bondage of Satan unto destruction and perdition. The bishop also recounts how God has restored the first natures in both man and creation, which occurred on the day when the Only-begotten Son took flesh, having been sent by God the Father, and redeemed man by his cross and his self-sacrifice, and raised him up again for eternal life. This life he now lives in the presence of the Father and the Son, and by the grace of the Holy Spirit.

Water itself, no longer an element of death, destruction, and bondage to Satan, has become revealed in its original nature, when it was revealed in the Jordan through the effect of the Holy Spirit, and later through the pierced side of Christ on the cross after he had died, in order to reveal that life proceeds from water after it was dead. The Holy Spirit descends on the water in baptism through the prayer of invocation by the bishop, in order for the water to be anointed with power from God, and for man to partake of his new communion with the Creator.

The Oil of Exorcism

After the consecration of the water, both the water and the baptized are anointed with the unmixed oil – the anointment with the oil of exorcism – and then the following prayer is said:

> O Master, who love men and who love souls,[7] God of mercy, pity and truth, we call on you for those who come to follow you, and we entrust them to the promises of your Only-begotten Son, who said:

---

[7] Cf. Wis 11:26

'Whose sins you shall forgive, they shall be forgiven them.' (Jn 20:23) We mark with this anointing these men and women who present themselves for this Divine regeneration. We beseech our Lord Jesus Christ to give them the power that heals and strengthens. Let him manifest himself through this anointing, let him remove from body, soul, or spirit every sign of sin, of iniquity, or the devil's action. Let him by his grace grant them forgiveness. Freed from sin, let them live for righteousness.[8] Now that they have become a new creation through this anointing and have been purified by this bath and renewed by the Spirit,[9] let them have the power henceforth to overcome all the hostile forces ranged against them and all the deceits of this life. Let them be gathered and reunited to the flock of the Lord and of our Savior Jesus Christ. Let them share with the saints the promised inheritance! Through him, glory to you and power, in the Holy Spirit, now and for ever and ever! Amen.[10]

The bishop pours oil in the water in the sign of the cross in order to frighten evil spirits. This is precisely why it is called an *exorcism*, that is the prayer of casting out evil spirits from matter and man, since water has been a dwelling place for evil spirits, and even man himself has been a prey to evil spirits. Nonetheless now, through man's salvation, matter itself is redeemed by the Holy Spirit in preparation for the more perfect redemption on the day of salvation.

After the water has been sanctified by the sign of the cross and the pouring of oil, it becomes a symbol of the glory of God, his presence, and the beginning of communion with him, just as he inaugurated this communion by his presence in the bread and wine of the Eucharist, granting us in it and through it true communion in him. "He who eats my flesh and drinks my blood abides in me, and I in him." (Jn 6:56) Whereas the descent of the Holy Spirit on Christ

---

[8] Cf. 1 Pet 2:24
[9] Cf. Titus 3:5
[10] Deiss, .202

marked the beginning of the time of salvation, the fullness of time, the descent of the Holy Spirit on the disciples marked the beginning of the time of salvation by the name of Christ in the person of the holy apostles. Likewise, also, the invocation of the Holy Spirit upon the water by the bishop in the name of Christ marks the time of salvation for the person baptized. Indeed, the entire congregation is a witness to this, and participates in the prayers.

The act of pouring oil in the water and anointing the baptized is the strongest sign of the work of salvation, which was accomplished by Christ on the cross and in his Resurrection. For just as one eats and drinks the bread and wine that have been transformed, and thus eats the body and drinks the blood of Christ, in the same manner the person is baptized by water and the Holy Spirit, and thus accepts communion and membership in the body of Christ. However, both the former and the latter are through a mystery and are not apparent. That is, they occur on the level of the work of the Holy Spirit, invisible and unseen. For this reason, baptism was the first mystery in the Church, while the revelation of that which is hidden waits until the day of salvation at the end of the world, when the material nature will cease to exist, and its true nature will be proclaimed in God.

The Holy Spirit and the White Garment

After anointing the entire body and all its organs with olive oil, the person is baptized in water three times, and rises to put on the Holy Spirit as he puts on the white garment. This white garment is called by the fathers the garment of righteousness, the bright robe, and the robe of the royal wedding, as John Chrysostom said.[11]

Scholars of liturgy have always maintained that this is one of the oldest rites in the Church, and occupies a special importance in the writings of the fathers. This is so because it reveals the effect, power, and efficacy of baptism, since the white robe is a symbol of spiritual purity, and it is "the robe of righteousness." (Is 61:10) On the other hand, the putting on the Spirit is not a symbol at all, but the essence of the baptismal liturgy, and the robe reveals this reality.

---

[11] *Baptismal Instructions,* ACW-31 (Mahwah, NY: Paulist Press, 1963), 67.

Indeed, the current state of dissolution, divisions, and the overall moral decline existing today is all because of an absence of the Holy Spirit. The early Church lived in the shadow of the work of the Holy Spirit that gathers the members of the one Church. The white robe was like the white linen ephod that David wore to converse with and consult God.[12] This robe is called the royal, priestly, and prophetic robe, and it is a fulfillment of the words of Peter, "But you are a chosen generation, a royal priesthood, a holy nation, his own special people, that you may proclaim the praises of him who called you out of darkness into his marvelous light." (1 Pet 2:9) This calling from darkness into light is a clear reference to baptism. Likewise in the book of Revelation it is written, "and has made us kings and priests to his God and Father." (Rev 1:6) Again, the robe of prophecy is referenced in Joel, "And also on my menservants and on my maidservants I will pour out my Spirit in those days," (Joel 2:29) as well as in Acts, "And on my menservants and on my maidservants I will pour out my Spirit in those days; And they shall prophesy." (Acts 2:18) Prophecy is not merely seeing the future, but proclaiming the Gospel in the present time. As radical as it may seem, loss of this royal, priestly, and prophetic role comes precisely from a loss of our awareness of the reality behind the white robe that was put on all of us on the day of our baptism.

The Seal of the Holy Spirit

A prayer for the chrism (*Myron*) by Serapion of Thmuis:

> God of the (heavenly) powers, help of every soul who turns to you and places himself under the powerful hand of your Only-begotten Son, we call on you: By the Divine and invisible power of the Lord and our Savior Jesus Christ, carry out through this oil your Divine and heavenly work. Those who have been baptized receive the anointing, (they are marked) with the impress of the sign of the saving cross of the Only-begotten Son. By this cross Satan

---

[12] Cf. 2 Sam 6:14 ; 1 Sam 30:7

and every hostile power have been defeated and are led captive in the triumphal procession. Regenerated and renewed by the bath of the new birth, let these here also share in the gifts of the Holy Spirit. Strengthened by the seal, let them remain 'steadfast and immovable,' (1 Cor 15:58) sheltered from all attack and pillaging, subjected neither to insult nor to aggression. Let them live to the very end in faith and the knowledge of the truth, in expectation of the hope of heavenly life and of the eternal promises of the Lord and our Savior Jesus Christ. Through him, glory to you and power, in the Holy Spirit, now and for ever and ever. Amen.[13]

St Paul says, "Now He who establishes us with you in Christ and has anointed us is God." (2 Cor 1:21) In fact, this verse is a commentary on the rite of chrismation. For after having been anointed with the regular (unmixed) oil, the immersion in water, the rising from water, and the putting on of the white garment, the person who is born again is now anointed with the holy chrism. This is an integral part of the sacrament of baptism, and the faith in general, as St Paul saw it.[14]

In Greek, the chrism or anointment is called χρἰσμα.[15] From this very word, came our own title as Christians, or those who are anointed with the Holy Spirit. Chrism is a grace that accompanies our lives and fulfills the work of baptism. However, there is no separation between baptism, the white robe, and chrismation. For while baptism is the gift of forgiveness of sins and the renewal of our creation as a second birth through the work of the Holy Spirit, in chrismation the soul receives from the inside the *personal* gift of the Holy Spirit, to dwell constantly in the life of the believer.

For this reason, the sacrament of chrismation imparts on baptism its efficacy in the interior life of the person, to be opened up to the Christian faith. In this sense, the Holy Spirit plays a future role in the

---

[13] Deiss, 204
[14] Cf. 2 Cor 1:21, 22 ; Eph 1:13
[15] Cf. 1 Jn 2:20, 27

life of the human being. In the early Church, chrismation was performed only by the laying on of apostolic hands. This is very clear in the baptism of the people of Samaria, who were not granted the Holy Spirit until Peter and John arrived and laid their hands on them. Thus, the chrism, which is the anointing with oil and perfumes handed down in the Church since the time of the apostles and Christ himself (in his burial), stands for the apostolic hands and even Christ's hands themselves.

At times, it is erroneously said that baptism grants the Holy Spirit. In fact, it is chrismation and the laying on of hands that does so. In fact, the very goal of baptism is that the catechumen is baptized with water *in order to* be anointed with the seal of chrism. Chrismation is also sometimes called the sacrament of confirmation (albeit mainly in Western circles), which is a renewal of the day of Pentecost. That is, the Spirit who descended on the disciples on the day of Pentecost now also descends on the baptized. For just as the Holy Spirit exists in Christ, so also it exists in the Christian, since Christ commands and exhorts that the Holy Spirit "will take of what is mine and declare it to you." (Jn 16:14)

When the baptized has received the seal of the inheritance of the kingdom, he immediately desires this kingdom and looks forward to it with all his strength, because the seal connects him mystically to the kingdom. The Holy Spirit that we receive is the seal for the day of redemption,[16] and the seal is the guarantee of our inheritance for the glory of God.[17] For this reason, the Holy Spirit is the hidden strength that pushes us towards repentance and a quick return to God. It is the fountain of sanctification in us, and the grace in which we stand.[18] It is also the proclaiming of the Trinity in whose communion we live, as St John says in his first epistle.[19] This is the Spirit that dwells in our temples,[20] which are counted as the temples of God,[21] made without hands. Thus, Christ finds his rest in us, and grants us the dominion of his kingship, the dignity of his priesthood, and the grace of his adoption. Christ has sealed us with the Spirit to become sacrifices to

---

[16] Cf. Eph 4:30
[17] Cf. Eph 1:14
[18] Cf. Rom 5:2
[19] Cf. 1 Jn 1:3
[20] Cf. 1 Cor 6:19
[21] Cf. 2 Cor 6:16

him, temple sacrifices ready for slaughter on his rational and heavenly altar.

Entering the Kingdom

On the feast of Pascha, after the baptized were sealed, and while wearing the white robes and their candles lit, they were led by the bishop along with the priests who participated in the baptism into the church. At that time, the entire congregation used to wait outside the doors of the church, also known as the royal or the main doors, waiting for the arrival of the baptismal procession and the beginning of the Eucharistic Liturgy. This baptismal procession was the climax of the sacrament of baptism. This procession started at the baptismal font in the form of a circle around it, while everyone sang what St Paul wrote in his epistle to the Galatians, "For as many of you as were baptized into Christ have put on Christ." (Gal 3:27) The procession then advances towards the church, led by the bishop, towards the closed royal doors. When they had arrived, the people let the baptized themselves open the royal doors, while the entire people chanted the antiphon that ended with the Paschal Troparion *Christ is Risen!* (Χριστός ἀνέστη).

Nowadays however, the people participate in the procession without any understanding of what it means. Some churches have retained some vestige of this procession at the entrance of the sanctuary, and when the baptized enter, the people participate in their procession around the church. However, the baptismal procession used to be the most important part of the Paschal celebration. The procession opened the door for everyone to enter the liturgical celebration, and the kingdom of God, since the Church is the kingdom of God on earth. In fact, the very *spirit* of the procession was in reaching the moment of *Christ is Risen!* which means participating in the Resurrection of Christ after all the rites of baptism and holy week. Finally, taking part in their first Eucharist provides those who were baptized the sustenance with the true food, needed on the journey to the perfect and eternal kingdom above.

All this ritual splendor has been lost, and its very image destroyed. Lost also is the true understanding of the Paschal liturgy, the baptismal procession, and the closed doors, which symbolized the closed doors of the kingdom in the face of Adam and his children. The entrance of the baptized dressed in white and carrying candles was a sign of their entrance into the royal wedding, prepared for those dressed appropriately. This royal wedding started with the Paschal liturgy, regarding which Gregory of Nyssa remarked that "it becomes brighter than the day"[22] Finally, the sacrament of baptism only ended with partaking of the Eucharist for the first time.

We have seen in this awesome and solemn rite the essential role of baptism in the Paschal liturgy. The setting aside of this specific day for baptism was extremely important, since Pascha occurs in what is known as *the new time* with regards to the Church and the people, on behalf of whom the feast is celebrated in the whole world. The people therefore comprehend the meaning of the feast as an inauguration of the new creation. In addition, the sacrament was performed at night, that is, in the midst of the dead time, rendering the meaning of baptism starkly clear and palpable in terms of its transfer from dead time to the lights of Pascha. For this reason, the church was illumined with lights more than the ordinary, and the feast of Pascha itself was called the Feast of Lights. In reality, it is the feast of *enlightenment* and the reopening of the way that Christ consecrated for us through the veil, that is his flesh,[23] and through the blood for entrance into the kingdom and the life of the age to come. That is the true and deepest meaning of receiving the baptized with "Christ is Risen!" which is the constantly renewed interpretation of baptism.

Now, the minds of the people have completely departed from what used to occur in the rite, even though the rite itself was an integral and well-explained part of the Resurrection and the meaning it carries, as we saw in this introductory explanation. Thus, baptism and its spiritual theology, together with the Church and the people, have all suffered from the absence of this rite, which contains the elements of faith and its practical interpretation.

However, thanks to God, the Church still preserved in her treasures all these early elements of the rite, and there is no reason these

---

[22] Cited by Schmemann, *Of Water and Spirit*, 113
[23] Cf. Heb 10:20

elements cannot be taught. This way, those who were baptized in infancy can still live this truth and depth. For all that was said above is in fact entrusted to the Church and to everyone who was ever baptized.

2

The Baptism of Christ

It is clear from Scripture and the history of the Church that baptism was first practiced on the day of Pentecost. This shows that baptism comes first through the impetus and work of the Holy Spirit, and his regeneration of human creation based on Christ's death and Resurrection. For this reason, Orthodoxy received baptism without question or suspicion throughout Christian history and until today, recognizing that the mystical and sacramental power of baptism stems from the Holy Spirit himself and his work in the Church.

All confusion and questions regarding baptism have already been presented in the person of Nicodemus in his dialogue with Christ. With his response, Christ presented to us baptism as a necessity and a Divine requirement, as a new birth from above, which is exactly the birth of water and the Spirit. In Christ, baptism is presented to us as something that cannot be analyzed or scrutinized, just as we cannot quite analyze or scrutinize the action of the wind, where it comes from and where it goes.

Having pointed to the role of the Holy Spirit in baptism, we now turn to the place of faith in Christ as a necessity and requirement for baptism. St Peter showed this clearly in his story with Cornelius. Having baptized Cornelius and his household, he explained his action to the Church saying, " 'If therefore God gave them the same gift as he gave us when we believed on the Lord Jesus Christ, who was I that I could withstand God?' When they heard these things they became silent; and they glorified God, saying, 'Then God has also granted to the gentiles repentance to life'." (Acts 11:17,18) We see in this story the core principle underlying baptism, faith in Christ, which is able to transcend any human limitations or strict ritual requirements.

In addition, something unique occurred in the story of Cornelius. That is, the descent of the Holy Spirit before baptism. This reversal of the common order occurred to convince Peter to baptize Cornelius and his household without any suspicion. Also, God acted in this way to help Peter transcend his pride and elitism, as well as to make clear to all the disciples in Jerusalem that it is he, not they, that has power to baptize. God alone has power to baptize, and knowing this, every person should be confident that his baptism comes from above and is performed by Christ himself. In this way, our birth from on high is indeed true and from God. In fact, faith in Christ's death and Resurrection is the very mystery underlying baptism. The descent of the Holy Spirit on Cornelius and his household before their baptism shows that God is not bound by rites or by any important person (whether a disciple or apostle). Christ has full and complete power over any rite.

Behind everyone who is baptized, stand Christ and his baptism in the Jordan, as well as his baptism in blood on the cross.[1] In this way, Christ's entrance into his kingdom after the Resurrection opened the door through which those who are baptized in his name enter. From this we should understand that salvation is granted not through rites and ceremonies, but through the work of Christ, who himself was baptized in the Jordan and on the cross. Baptism therefore is true *kerygma*, a practical realization of the teaching of the apostles in the form of a response, an act of faith. Baptism is the practical expression of the faith in all its elements; an act of faith first and foremost in Christ himself and his saving power.

Baptism is the only seal a Christian receives to form a unique Christian unity, and become a member of Christ, in the one body of the Church. In reality, baptism is a process of grafting the bitter olive branch unto the Divine body, so that everyone may acquire the same mind of Christ, his life, and draw from him the very elements of eternal life.

The baptism of Christ was the dividing event between the Old Testament and the New Testament, which Christ inaugurated the day he was baptized. Therefore, the baptism of Christ is the beginning of the gospel. When Christ was anointed with the Holy Spirit in his baptism, his ministry started. Thus, baptism is the beginning of man's

---

[1] "But I have a baptism (βάπτισμα) to be baptized with, and how distressed I am till it is accomplished." (Lk 12:50)

ministry and Divine calling, as well as his return to the bosom of God. The story of Christ's baptism contains certain elements that form some of the essential foundations of the sacrament of baptism.

One of these elements is Christ's saying to John the Baptist, when the latter shied at first from baptizing him, "Permit it to be so now, for thus it is fitting for us to fulfill all righteousness." (Mt 3:15) Righteousness here refers to Christ's mission in returning and fulfilling man's righteousness in the eyes of God, which by necessity includes forgiveness of sins and reconciliation with God. In addition, the voice of the Father from heaven addressing Christ and saying "You are my beloved Son in whom I am well-pleased" (Mt 3:17) was addressed to all of humanity in the person of Jesus Christ. Forgiveness and adoption, therefore, are two of the fundamental elements of Christ's baptism, and by consequence, our own baptism.

The Church, taking these elements as a model, and building on the foundation of Christ's baptism in the Jordan, applied all what she learned from Christ's baptism through her own baptism. The baptism of Christ presents adoption, anointing by the Holy Spirit, and grants the power and gift to wrestle with Satan, opening the way before man. Through baptism, the Church also grants entrance into the life and mind of Christ, and thus, to unity with him and the right of entering with him into the kingdom.

The Church accepted with confidence the meaning of the descent of the Holy Spirit on Christ in the Jordan. This happened in order to sanctify the water, and radically transform it into living water, able to make alive, and possess the power to put into effect the words of Christ, "born of water and the Spirit," (Jn 3:5) just as the transformation of bread and wine through the prayer of invocation (ἐπίκλησις) is ultimately done for the transformation and radical revival of man himself. Now, we can begin to understand that the baptism of Christ in the Jordan was the Divine entrance, visible and yet mystical, that allows the world and man himself to enter into a spiritual renewal. The Church understood this theologically regarding the Lord's saying after the Resurrection, "And Jesus came and spoke to them, saying, 'All authority has been given to me in heaven and on earth'," (Mt 28:18) meaning that all powers and elements in heaven and on earth have come under his dominion and are made ready for the transformation to come.

THE BIRTH FROM ON HIGH

This happened after Christ fulfilled his own baptism through death and the baptism of blood on the cross, fulfilling the meaning, breadth and depth of the baptism of the Jordan. Having done this, he presented to the Church the complete meaning of baptism, both as birth-giving and as a sacrifice through death. Thus, the baptism of the Church became both for life and death, or in the likeness of Christ's death and Resurrection; death to sin, and life to God; death with Christ and life with Christ.

Gradually, all these unique meanings in the rite of baptism entered into the Church's theological teaching, since what occurred in baptism was the basis of theological teaching in the Church among the saintly disciples, St Paul, and the rest of the fathers. Indeed, may the reader understand this as well, for this is the very reason why I wrote this study on baptism, since unfortunately the Church and the people have forgotten that what happened in the baptism of Christ is the very foundation of theology and spiritual-theological knowledge in the Church. For example, St Peter says, and in fact describes what occurs in baptism, "For Christ also suffered once for sins, the just for the unjust, that he might bring us to God, being put to death in the flesh but made alive by the Spirit." (I Pet 3:18)

Furthermore, St John the Evangelist gives us in his gospel a real and tangible image of the issuing of water and blood from the side of Christ after he died on the cross. St John uses this image as the source and origin of both baptism and the Eucharist, the two fundamental sacraments of the Church. In this manner, the Church issues forth and is born from the side of Christ, like Eve coming forth from the side of Adam. The early fathers saw in this the idea that the baptism of Christ in death, his baptism of blood, handed down to us the sacrament of our baptism, built on the foundation of the death of Christ. It is known that man gained all spiritual gifts and talents by the death of Christ, the most important of which is the forgiveness of sins, and the greatest of which is the ability to enter the kingdom of God. St Paul extrapolated from this saying, "as many of us as were baptized into Christ Jesus were baptized into his death. Therefore we were buried with him through baptism into death, that just as Christ was raised from the dead by the glory of the Father, even so we also should walk in newness of life. For if we have been united together in the likeness of his death, certainly we also shall be in the likeness of his Resurrection." (Rom 6:3-5) Based on the baptism of Christ, whether in the Jordan or on the cross, water carries the double meaning of death and its dominion, as well as power and triumph over it.

3

From the Jordan to Golgotha

In the book of Acts, Luke recounts the story of choosing a replacement to Judas the traitor. One of the conditions required of this potential disciple was that he be a contemporary of Christ, "beginning from the baptism of John to that day when he was taken up from us." (Acts 1:22) This condition is very important, and it highlights the two critical moments in the history of Christ's ministry. Taking Christ's baptism and ascension, we are presented with a framework for preaching and proclaiming Christ the Savior, because baptism and ascension are the beginning and the end of Christ's ministry on earth. Thus, the baptism of Christ, from the perspective of the apostles, leads up to the ascension as its ultimate conclusion, and is therefore a critical event of salvation history. Christ's baptism and ascension reveal the powerful work of the Father in Christ Jesus. From this point begins the theology of baptism.

Baptism entered the teaching the apostles as a foundation of their preaching, their *kerygma*. The rite of baptism took root in the Church as the beginning of Christ's ministry, and because of Christ's baptism we became able to imitate Christ. Not only that, but baptism became at once connection to the past, as the beginning of the new Christian creation, and a connection to the future as the *eschaton*, the ultimate end of salvation, redemption, and all the works of Christ. Thus, the two poles of the theology of baptism are understood as the baptism of Christ in the Jordan, and his ascension.

However, the Lord emphasized that the baptism of John itself with its characteristics would not remain as it is. By Christ's participation in the baptism of John, he placed the final barrier between the baptism of the past and the future baptism of the Spirit, "for John truly baptized with water, but you shall be baptized with the Holy

Spirit not many days from now." (Acts 1:5) This provides a clear picture that the baptism of John has ended, only to be refashioned anew and with remarkable perfection. If the baptism of John was from heaven, Christian baptism is heaven itself, being a rebirth from above.[1] This is the perfection concerning which the Lord said, "It is fitting for us to *fulfill* all righteousness." (Mt 3:15) Christianity proceeded forth from baptism with water, which Christ accepted in the Jordan to build the future new baptism.

The baptism of Christ – as opposed to that of John – is unique precisely because it is fulfilled and perfected on the cross. Even though Christ's baptism was *eschatological*, looking forward to the *eschaton*, proclaiming and inaugurating the mystery of the age to come, nonetheless Christ's words "It is fitting for us to fulfill all righteousness" were only perfected and accomplished when he carried the sins of the world on the cross. In other words, baptism took its final seal in blood, "I have a baptism to be baptized with."(Lk 12:50) Thus, baptism started with water and the laying on of hands for prophecy, and was concluded with blood and the Father laying on his own hand, since the righteousness, which Christ pointed out at his baptism, was fulfilled and perfected in the baptism of death; "that he might be just and the justifier of the one who has faith in Jesus." (Rom 3:26) Following baptism as the beginning of righteousness, the cross and the Resurrection were the fulfillment of all righteousness. From the cross and the Resurrection was born the new man as a new creation that has crossed the water with Christ and has been dyed in blood on the cross with him, and thus was renewed and has put on his original perfect image in God. In short, the baptism of water is unto washing of sins, while the baptism of blood is unto sanctification, for him who was offered on the cross became a living and rational sacrifice for the expiation of the sins of the people. Thus, the baptism of water achieved the perfection of its heavenly form and its Divine reality from the sacrifice of Christ on the cross, while the true inauguration of the Christian person was accomplished through the Resurrection and ascension, since Christian baptism itself took its efficacy from the ascension of the Lord and the appearance of the new man. This is

---

[1] Cf. Jn 3:3

because baptism is the new Christian birth of man, founded on the work of Christ in forgiveness of sins.

Accordingly, baptism contains the act of forgiveness of sins, entering the kingdom of heaven and obtaining the gift of the Holy Spirit. St Paul summarizes it thus, "as many of us as were baptized into Christ Jesus were baptized into his death. Therefore we were buried with him through baptism into death, that just as Christ was raised from the dead by the glory of the Father, even so we also should walk in newness of life." (Rom 6:3,4) However, the forgiveness of sins in baptism does not occur through the outward act of Christ's baptism in the Jordan, but from its effect and essence, which stem from the work of his sacrifice of death, his Resurrection, and our partaking of this death and this Resurrection unto the inheritance of a new life.

In fact, the book of Acts derives the value of forgiveness of sins in baptism from its understanding of the baptism of Christ in the Jordan, though slowly and eventually, the light of the Resurrection itself was proclaimed as a beginning of eternal life. Consequently, the light of the Resurrection was reflected on baptism to imbue it with an expiatory theology through partaking of death and Resurrection in Christ, which St Paul highly praised in his epistles.[2]

Nonetheless, the baptism of John unto repentance and forgiveness of sins was in its reality and eschatological understanding an entry into the age of the Messiah, which was God's intention for it. Through Christ's acceptance of this baptism, he made it truly an entryway to him.

Based on this, the Church grants through baptism the mystery of entering into the life of the Trinity, "the life was manifested, and we have seen, and bear witness, and declare to you that eternal life which was with the Father and was manifested to us... and truly our fellowship is with the Father and with his Son Jesus Christ." (I Jn 1:2,3) Having obtained life and fellowship with the Father and the Son, we have become partakers of Christ's death and Resurrection, which means we are united with the crucified and risen Christ with a unity vivified by the Spirit. This unity or union in Christ that those who are baptized obtain is what worthily grants them the title of *saints*, which

---

[2] Cf. Rom 6:3,4

Paul uses to address them in most of his epistles, "Paul, an apostle of Jesus Christ by the will of God, and Timothy our brother, to the saints and faithful brethren in Christ who are in Colosse." (Col 1:1,2)

In fact, this unity with Christ in baptism through faith and belief in his death and Resurrection, originates first and foremost from the union of the Son of God with flesh – man's flesh – a complete and total union, without mingling, confusion, or alteration. This means that he became united with us totally and completely, so that in the end, after we have received forgiveness of our sins, we can be born again a new spiritual creation, ready for the same union by which he was united with us, so that we may be united with him, having partaken with him in his death and Resurrection, since his body is our body. Keep in mind that this partaking is not just in baptism, but it is first and foremost the result of his union with us since his birth, which became our birth. After that, his death became our death, and his Resurrection became our resurrection. In short, Christ is the one that fashioned our union with him, without our will or worthiness, since we were dead and without will.

In the end, we go beyond mind and logic when we say that we are united with the body of Christ, though it truly occurs. Nonetheless, he himself utterly surpassed all mind and logic when he – God the omnipotent – descended from heaven and was united with our flesh. Is this possible? Is this not the largest stumbling block of all? For our union with Christ was made possible through his union with us.

Returning to baptism – the reason behind this incredible mystical relationship – we see that the divine and mystical work of baptism gathered us as members in the body of Christ, as Paul the apostle says, "For by one Spirit we were all baptized into one body," (1 Cor 12:13) and thus, all those who are saved and redeemed are gathered together in it. This is the meaning of the Church! This is the sacramental meaning, which we practice both in baptism and the Eucharist. Paul the apostle expresses this reality when he says, "Till we all come to the unity of the faith and of the knowledge of the Son of God, to a perfect man, to the measure of the stature of the fullness of Christ." (Eph 4:13) However, baptism alone does not grant this fullness of Christ. Instead, it places the seed, and we, through the help of the Holy Spirit, nourish and cultivate this seed to develop into a mighty tree. Nonetheless, in its origin, baptism remains a small seed. This is the wonderful and joyful theology of baptism, which was fulfilled and perfected in Golgotha, and which we too must perfect in our own lives in the likeness of his death.

> For if we have been united together in the likeness of his death, certainly we also shall be in the likeness of his Resurrection. (Rom 6:5)

> Now if we died with Christ, we believe that we shall also live with him. (Rom 6:8)

In order to understand how this happens, we must start step by step. First, what is the kind of death that Christ suffered? What is the kind of death that we are called on to experience in baptism? We have to know, before anything else, that the death of Christ was a voluntary act. Christ willed and desired to die as we can see in the following verse:

> Therefore my Father loves me, because I lay down my life that I may take it again. No one takes it from me, but I lay it down of myself. I have power to lay it down, and I have power to take it again. This command I have received from my Father. (Jn 10:17,18)

Our faith asserts that Christ, in his Divine nature, was not subject to death. This means that Christ was free from death, its causes, and its consequences. Christ is the Life, so that when he died, he did so voluntarily. Christ's death was the death of him who is immortal, him who is not liable to death. This is what made his death a salvific act suffered for others.

What does it mean that Christ desired to die? This revolves around the spiritual meaning of death and its content. Death, in terms of its original reality, is spiritual and not simply physical. This is true even though the general understanding of death among people is merely physical and bodily, as a necessary end of life on earth. However, faith transcends this end and asserts the existence of another, eternal life, which is the life of the immortal soul. With this meaning in mind, death becomes a crossing over from a dead life to an undying life. Note also that death belongs to the flesh, while immortality belongs to the soul.

A weak Christian view of death is that of the death of the flesh, even though the Christian sometimes tastes of spiritual death while alive, and it is indeed our goal to be free of death even while lying in the tomb! Thus, real death is spiritual death, and not physical or fleshly death. With regards to Adam, death was a separation from God, the source of life, the giver of life, and life itself.

This life, God's life, or God who is life, is as St John says, "the light of men." (Jn 1:4) When man refuses this life, through transgression and lack of submission and obedience, he dies an eternal death, since the life he rejected was eternal. Thus, the original sin was an eternal spiritual death, which takes the form of physical death on earth. For death is not an organic state, but a spiritual reality caused by sin. St Paul called it a sting, in the likeness of a scorpion's deadly sting.[1]

When the first man refused the real life, the only reality that God gave him as a gift, sin entered into the world and death was through sin.[2] There is no other life but God's life, and whoever refuses it must die even if he lives. Life without God is death, and this is the spiritual death. Even if man lives after having refused the true life from the hands of God, his life or earthly existence will be filled with death, for he lives in a state of continuous separation from God. In this way, man isolates himself, is overwhelmed with fear, and is filled with enmity. He submits to the slavery of sin, and consequently to all of matter. Finally, his life loses all meaning and he becomes surrounded by desire, emptiness, and finally death.

As long as we are unable to acquire this Christian vision and true awareness and understanding of death, as a law of terror and sin that fills life with death that reigns over the world,[3] we remain unable to understand the true value of Christ's death for us and for the whole world. This is because the natural, physical death is in fact the bitter fruit of spiritual death, from which Christ came to save us. Herein lies the difficult meaning of Christ's voluntary death in the fullness of his free will. For Christ chose to accomplish his own death, because he

---

[1] Cf. I Cor 15:56
[2] Cf. Rom 5:12
[3] Cf. Rom 5:14

loved the Father more than himself, whereas man died because he desired life for himself, loving himself more than God.

For inasmuch as man's love for himself and his life was the main cause of his sin, which is the bitter root of death, Christ's sacrifice and offering his life became therefore the main cause of man's salvation from sin, and his setting free from spiritual death. Christ's desire and will to die is then considered the first and foremost act of perfect love of the Father and man (in the person of Christ), in total and perfect obedience to the will of the Father. In other words, Christ's death had no motive in itself other than love. His death was the ultimate proclamation of love, in order to remove the sting of death, which is sin, and to free man from the dominion of death.

Christ did not eliminate physical death. Had he done so, he would have effectively destroyed the world itself, insofar as death is in the world and reigns over it. It is true that death is not part of the world, but it is the basis of life in the world, since everyone that lives in the world lives towards death. However, what Christ accomplished was far greater. He annulled the sting of death, which is sin, and consequently annulled death as a spiritual reality. He did this by putting on death and filling it with his presence, his life, and his love. By doing so, he changed death from being a separation from God and the cause of corruption for man and the world, to a joyous and bright passageway, enlightened with the fullness of love and eternal life. "For to me, to live is Christ, and to die is gain." (Phil 1:21) St Paul here is not speaking of the death of the flesh, but about death in its new meaning; death with Christ the symbol of power and victory, because those who believe in Christ and live in him no longer experience death. Death was swallowed up in victory by their faith.[4] Thus, every tomb of every saint became full of life instead of death.

Now, what is the meaning of "if we have been united together in the likeness of his death, certainly we also shall be in the likeness of his Resurrection" (Rom 6:5)? What is the meaning of *likeness*? It means that we must follow in the footsteps of Christ, and have fellowship with him through faith in him and love of him. In this way, our will becomes his will, and our faith becomes not simply a confession or even acquisition of what is his, but above all else an offering

---

[4] Cf. I Cor 15:54

to him of our lives and souls. This is the meaning of his commandment, "*you* follow me." (Jn 21:22) There is no other way for us to believe in him other than to accept his faith as *our* faith, and to accept his love as *our* love, and his will as *our* will. Faith in Christ means all of Christ, and outside of him there is no faith. By all of Christ is meant his obedience, his love, and his will, by which we come to know him, and through which he causes himself to shine on us.

Thus, if we believe in what he does not believe, love what he does not love, will what he does not will, or obey what he does not obey, then we no longer believe in him, having separated him from our life! Yet, we still claim to live on the hope of miracles, and cry for help without actually doing what he does, but instead we obey a will other than his, and still call him *Lord*, and worship him without fulfilling his will. This is not faith in him! For we were not saved because we believed in miracles and supernatural powers. This is faith he does not desire, because it is a superstitious and false faith!

On the other hand, if we conform our will to his will, which fills his life and has led him to death in order to destroy it, this is rightly called faith. This is the *likeness* of Christ and his works. For if we imitate his death, surely we will imitate his Resurrection, since his death results in Resurrection.

It is also impossible to believe in Christ without actually desiring the cup that he tasted, and to be baptized with the baptism by which he was baptized. That is, to enter into a fierce combat against sin, and to place ourselves where he is. This is the likeness of Christ's death, this is the true faith, "faith in the Son of God, who loved me and gave himself for me," (Gal 2:20) and loved the Church and gave himself up for her. If we live far away from imitating him and loyalty to his life, it is not true faith, but a theoretical knowledge that we received and memorized to repeat far away from our hearts, our consciousness and our true faith.

Based on this, the baptism we speak of becomes the baptism of his death and Resurrection, which we desire and seek after. This is because he himself has desired and sought after death, changing it to new and eternal life.

4

The Holy Spirit and Christ's Death and Resurrection

There is a fundamental difference between the baptism of John and Christian baptism, as was shown in the previous chapters. The focus of this chapter is to show the unique presence of the Holy Spirit in the baptism of Christ. This John the Baptist himself affirms saying, "I indeed baptize you with water unto repentance, but he who is coming after me is mightier than I, whose sandals I am not worthy to carry. He will baptize you with the Holy Spirit and fire," (Mt 3:11) and also, "I indeed baptize you with water; but one mightier than I is coming, whose sandal strap I am not worthy to loose. He will baptize you with the Holy Spirit and fire," (Lk 3:16) and "I indeed baptized you with water, but he will baptize you with the Holy Spirit." (Mk 1:8) In these verses, fire is a sign of the frightful judgment, which will be the penalty for whoever does not receive baptism. From all this we can see that the baptism of John is unlike the baptism of Christ, for the latter is not a preparation for some future grace. The baptism of Christ is a baptism of perfection and fulfillment, and leads directly to the kingdom of heaven, of which John the Baptist came to prepare the way.

The sending of the Holy Spirit that Christ spoke of,[1] and has already fulfilled on the day of Pentecost confirming his power and work, is an eschatological act concerned with revealing the kingdom of God and granting the power to reach it. It is an eschatological gift, though it requires our cooperation and acceptance of it. This is why Mark was content with mentioning only the Holy Spirit, choosing not to mention fire since fire does not follow the present age. This eschatological aspect apparent in the baptism of Christ is completely new,

---

[1] Cf. Acts 1:5,8

and is not to be found in the understanding of baptism of John or in the Old Testament. Thus, the gift of baptism is not derived from this or some other past event, but directly from the person of Christ and his work.

The pouring out of the Holy Spirit on all flesh[2] is an act exclusive to the name of Christ, "whom the Father will send in my name," (Jn 14:26) as well to Christ's Resurrection and ascension to the Father. We can see this from the words of Christ himself, "for if I do not go away, the helper will not come to you; but if I depart, I will send him to you." (Jn 16:7) For this reason, the Church did not start baptizing the believers until she became the house of the Holy Spirit and capable of bestowing him, knowing that he is sent from the Father in the name of Christ: "But the helper, the Holy Spirit, whom the Father will send in my name, He will teach you all things, and bring to your remembrance all things that I said to you." (Jn 14:26)

The forgiveness of sins that John preached was based on belief that this baptism was from heaven. Nonetheless, the power and efficacy of this forgiveness did not go beyond the body and time, because it was merely a preparation for a coming age and not for eternal life. On the other hand, the baptism of Christ is connected with faith in Christ himself, and what he has done for salvation, that is, forgiveness of sins through his death, burial, and Resurrection. Forgiveness here is neither temporal nor bodily, but an eternal forgiveness, centered around the soul first and foremost. Thus, the baptism of Christ came to be based primarily on faith in the person of Christ, and the message of salvation that was accomplished through his death, burial, and Resurrection. All this was revealed to John the Baptist, as a prophet and forerunner of Christ, so when he saw Christ after his baptism walking near the Jordan he said, "Behold! The Lamb of God who takes away the sin of the world!" (Jn 1:29) For Christ descended into the Jordan to accomplish this great mission, which he called the fulfillment of every righteousness, not for his own sake but for the sake of us all. The righteousness of all is the lifting off of their sins, for no one is considered righteous unless they are without sin.

We again reiterate that the newness of baptism is the pouring out of the Holy Spirit, the gift of the Father in the name of Christ, which

---

[2] Cf. Acts 2:17

was poured after Christ's ascension, "But the helper, the Holy Spirit, whom the Father will send in my name, he will teach you all things," (Jn 14:26) "Nevertheless I tell you the truth. It is to your advantage that I go away; for if I do not go away, the helper will not come to you; but if I depart, I will send him to you," (Jn. 16:7), and also, "for the Holy Spirit was not yet given, because Jesus was not yet glorified" (Jn 7:39) Christ indeed fulfilled his promise, for ten days after his ascension, on the feast of Pentecost, he poured out the Holy Spirit. In baptism, forgiveness of sins is accomplished based on participating with Christ in his death and Resurrection through faith and immersion in water, in the likeness of dying and rising again with him. Herein is the work of the Holy Spirit in vivifying or raising us from the dead to rise with Christ, since the Holy Spirit forms the image of the second birth from water, so that the new man is born again in the image of his creator in the glory of the Resurrection, and thus obtains eternal life.

For this reason, the work of the Holy Spirit in baptism became an essential act of fulfillment, without which baptism itself is not accomplished. In other words, the work of baptism itself became the granting of the Holy Spirit after the forgiveness of sins. Then the Holy Spirit again completes the work of baptism in the rising of the newly born in the image of Christ unto the fullness of eternal life. For baptism with water is death and forgiveness, and baptism with water is Resurrection and life, and thus all in all, the baptism with water and the Spirit becomes the entrance into the kingdom of God in Christ.

This is explained by the words of St Paul, "Or do you not know that as many of us as were baptized into Christ Jesus were baptized into his death? Therefore we were buried with him through baptism into death, that just as Christ was raised from the dead by the glory of the Father, even so we also should walk in newness of life. For if we have been united together in the likeness of his death, certainly we also shall be in the likeness of his Resurrection." (Rom 6:3-5)

Here, the expression *in the likeness of his death* refers to the difference between his death and ours. For his death was a dying to sin, whereas our death is a death of the flesh of sin. And just as Christ died once and rose, and death will no longer have dominion over him,[3] likewise also, according to the epistle to the Hebrews, our baptism is one only since our participation in the death of the cross happens once and for all. Thus, if someone falls away from the faith after baptism, he cannot be renewed once again, or else he would be crucifying for himself the Son of God again.[4]

> For to which of the angels did he ever say: ' You are my Son, *today I have begotten you?*'. (Heb 1:5)
>
> So also Christ did not glorify himself to become high priest, but it was he who said to him: ' You are my Son, today *I have begotten you*'." (Heb 5:5)

If we add to this the testimony of Luke that appears in some western manuscripts, "You are my beloved Son, today I have begotten you," (Lk 3:22) we can see even more clearly the veracity of what Paul said in these verses. This is considered to be of the utmost importance to the messianic understanding of Jesus Christ regarding his Resurrection from the dead. Both of these references from Hebrews refer to the psalm, "I will declare the decree the Lord has said to me, 'You are my Son, today I have begotten You." (Ps 2:7) This was explained by Paul that *today I have begotten you* is the day of his Resurrection,[5] and was also echoed in Acts "And we declare to you glad tidings—that promise which was made to the fathers. God has fulfilled this for us their children, in that he has raised up Jesus. As it is also written in the second psalm: ' You are my Son, today I have begotten you'," (Acts 13:32-34) taking the entire biblical witness on these verses, we can truly begin to understand the mystery of the Resurrection as it relates to the new birth.

The link between the Resurrection and the new birth is a theological expression of the utmost importance. The Resurrection is a new heavenly birth,[6] and the scriptures are very clear, "God has fulfilled this for us their children, in that he has raised up Jesus. As it is also written in the second psalm: ' You are my Son, today I have begotten You', And that he raised him from the dead, no more to return

---

[3] Cf. Rom 6:9,10
[4] Cf. Heb 6:6
[5] Cf. Rom 1:4, Heb 5:5
[6] Cf. Acts 13:33

to corruption." (Acts 13:32-34) In this way, we understand baptism to be a second birth, a new birth, firmly based on the death of Christ and his Resurrection. The Resurrection of Christ, in its theological reality, is a new birth from heaven, that is, from above as we all heard in God's calling from heaven at the time of Christ's baptism. The Resurrection is also a new birth from heaven considering that the Resurrection of Christ is a new birth for all of humanity in him after dying with him. "Blessed be the God and Father of our Lord Jesus Christ, who according to his abundant mercy has begotten us again to a living hope through the Resurrection of Jesus Christ from the dead." (I Pet 1:3)

5

Baptism and Unity with the Body of Christ

When Christ died, he "bore our sins in his own body on the tree, that we, having died to sins, might live for righteousness." (I Pet 2:24). On our part, we died with him since the flesh he took was our flesh, and he tasted death because he carried our sins. He died for us, and we died with him as well. After the cross, he was buried three days, and we were still with him, dead in the flesh of sin. Likewise, when he rose from the dead, he did so with our flesh through the power of his divinity, his will, raising us with him. He rose through his eternal holiness that is without sin, so we benefited from his holiness. Thereby, we entered into a unity with him that was accomplished through his incarnation, death, and Resurrection.

Christ had hinted before that his death on the cross and the shedding of his blood would in fact be his baptism, which he would necessarily pass through on our behalf. So what does this mean? It means that, along with Christ's shedding of blood or his baptism, we accepted our own baptism by necessity. This means that we were baptized with Christ in his death and Resurrection, through no act of our own, no faith, no power of any kind, since he accomplished all this before we came to realize:

> Even when we were dead in trespasses, [God] made us alive together with Christ. (Eph 2:5)

> For God so loved the world that he gave his only begotten Son, that whoever believes in him should not perish but have everlasting life. (Jn 3:16)

> But God demonstrates his own love toward us, in that while we were still sinners, Christ died for us. (Rom 5:8)

It is a one-sided act, free of charge. The baptism of Christ which he accepted through his shedding of blood on the cross is the only authentic theological understanding of the work of baptism.

Through our journey to research and understand baptism, a question might be asked: Was Christ baptized, and did he shed his blood, die, and rise again from the dead for the sake of every human being? Here, we return once more to the expression of Paul in his epistle to the Romans,

> Or do you not know that as many of us as were baptized into Christ Jesus were baptized into his death? Therefore we were buried with him through baptism into death, that just as Christ was raised from the dead by the glory of the Father, even so we also should walk in newness of life. For if we have been united together in the likeness of his death, certainly we also shall be in the likeness of his Resurrection. (Rom 6:3-5)

If we add to this what Paul wrote in his first epistle to the Corinthians, "For by one Spirit we were all baptized into one body—whether Jews or Greeks, whether slaves or free—and have all been made to drink into one Spirit," (I Cor 12:13) we can begin to understand that our participation in the death of Christ and his Resurrection in baptism occurs *in one Spirit, into one body*. It is clear that the body of Christ is meant here in an ecclesiological sense, that is, the community of believers or the Church. This body of Christ is the body crucified on the cross, as well as the risen (and therefore glorified) body, which we were all called to become members thereof. This we can see in the following verses:

> I now rejoice in my sufferings for you, and fill up in my flesh what is lacking in the afflictions of Christ, for the sake of his body, which is the church. (Col 1:24)

> For as the sufferings of Christ abound in us, so our consolation also abounds through Christ. (II Cor 1:5)

> But rejoice to the extent that you partake of Christ's sufferings, that when his glory is revealed, you may also be glad with exceeding joy. (I Pet 4:13)
>
> But now Christ is risen from the dead, and has become the firstfruits of those who have fallen asleep. For since by man came death, by man also came the Resurrection of the dead. For as in Adam all die, even so in Christ all shall be made alive. (I Cor 15:20-22)

Thus, based on the one hand on a relationship with Christ in his death and Resurrection, and on the other hand on building the community of believers in Christ, Paul writes to Galatia,

> For as many of you as were baptized into Christ have put on Christ. There is neither Jew nor Greek, there is neither slave nor free, there is neither male nor female; for you are all one in Christ Jesus. And if you are Christ's, then you are Abraham's seed, and heirs according to the promise. (Gal 3:27-29)

In all these verses, we do not read about how the baptized can *understand* their relationship with Christ's death and Resurrection. Rather, the baptized person accepts and receives with his mind, his heart, his intellect, his spirit, his faith, and all his being a living relationship, a connection, a cleaving, and a unity in the death and Resurrection of Christ, and consequently his body, in order to become a living member of that body through death. Having done this, his sins are lifted immediately, and through the Resurrection he accepts his new personhood, a new living creation according to the image of the risen Christ.

In short, the human being exists in a state of open acceptance of divine action. Christ is in a continuous state of accepting new members to his body, which embraces the entire universe. Ultimately, God is the one that unites new members to the body of Christ in the sacrament of baptism.

> And the Lord added to the church daily those who were being saved. (Acts 2:47)

> Then those who gladly received his word were baptized; and that day about three thousand souls were added to them. (Acts 2:41)

Needless to say, it is the Church's role to proclaim, praise, and preach this in her teachings. But does the teaching of the Church truly show how she is built? Or is it God in fact who builds her secretly and mystically through the work of faith and baptism? Is it in fact for the Church to proclaim this? And, most importantly, is there joy and happiness in proclaiming this? The Scriptures communicate unequivocally this vibrant sense of joy,

> But God demonstrates his own love toward us, in that while we were still sinners, Christ died for us. Much more then, having now been justified by his blood, we shall be saved from wrath through him. For if when we were enemies we were reconciled to God through the death of his Son, much more, having been reconciled, we shall be saved by his life. (Rom 5:8-10)

> In this is love, not that we loved God, but that he loved us and sent his Son to be the propitiation for our sins…We love him because he first loved us. (I Jn 4:10,19)

> You did not choose me, but I chose you and appointed you that you should go and bear fruit, and that your fruit should remain, that whatever you ask the Father in my name he may give you. (Jn 15:16)

This is all accomplished first of all through baptism. Baptism has gathered us, and united us in the body of Christ. For the grace of baptism is not merely an image to be contemplated, or to be spoken about, but a living and vibrant reality; we draw on its vibrancy from Golgotha, which was accomplished once and for all. This reality extends through baptism into the depths of time, while Golgotha itself will remain a one-time event, just as it is in the Eucharist. This does not mean that baptism is a repetition of Golgotha, for Golgotha will remain a *new* event forever, and those who are baptized renew it in their minds and in the Church.

Baptism and Unity with the Body of Christ

6

Baptism and Faith

The importance of baptism rests on two points. First, the act of baptism itself, and second, the results of baptism, that which remains for the rest of a person's life. And now, we must lay the foundation and ask, what is the role of faith in baptism? And what is the role of faith after baptism? Here, we must clarify what is written in Paul's first epistle to the Corinthians:

> Moreover, brethren, I do not want you to be unaware that all our fathers were under the cloud, all passed through the sea, all were baptized into Moses in the cloud and in the sea, all ate the same spiritual food, and all drank the same spiritual drink. For they drank of that spiritual rock that followed them, and that rock was Christ. But with most of them God was not well pleased, for their bodies were scattered in the wilderness. Now these things became our examples, to the intent that we should not lust after evil things as they also lusted. And do not become idolators as were some of them. As it is written, 'the people sat down to eat and drink, and rose up to play.' Nor let us commit sexual immorality, as some of them did, and in one day twenty-three thousand fell; nor let us tempt Christ, as some of them also tempted, and were destroyed by serpents; nor complain, as some of them also complained, and were destroyed by the destroyer. Now all these things happened to them as examples, and they were written for our admonition, upon whom the ends of the ages have come." (I Cor 1:1-11)

Paul is encouraging us, along with his Corinthian audience, to closely examine what happened to the people of Israel on their journey to the Red Sea, a classic example of baptism. This incident was mentioned again in Scripture together with its catastrophic results in another of Paul's epistles.[1] We read elsewhere in the New Testament regarding falling away from the grace of baptism:

> For it is impossible for those who were once enlightened, and have tasted the heavenly gift, and have become partakers of the Holy Spirit, and have tasted the good word of God and the powers of the age to come, if they fall away, to renew them again to repentance, since they crucify again for themselves the Son of God, and put him to an open shame. (Heb 6:4-6)

And also,

> For if we sin willfully after we have received the knowledge of the truth, there no longer remains a sacrifice for sins, but a certain fearful expectation of judgment, and fiery indignation which will devour the adversaries. Anyone who has rejected Moses' law dies without mercy on the testimony of two or three witnesses. Of how much worse punishment, do you suppose, will he be thought worthy who has trampled the Son of God underfoot, counted the blood of the covenant by which he was sanctified a common thing, and insulted the Spirit of grace? For we know him who said, 'Vengeance is mine, I will repay', says the Lord. And again, 'The Lord will judge his people.' It is a fearful thing to fall into the hands of the living God. (Heb 10:26-31)

Clearly, the grace of baptism cannot be replaced. To him who loses this grace, life becomes highly precarious, compared to what he had initially received in baptism. At the same time, we find that what is

---

[1] Cf. Heb. 3:7-13

granted in baptism is a great gift, surpassing all intellect and imagination, and stands in no need of understanding. It is membership in the body of Christ, and therefore a heavenly citizenship. Any reversal or halting in the grace of baptism is counted as treason, just like betraying one's homeland.

Baptism as an act of salvation is only the beginning, hence why it is called a second birth. But birth is the beginning of a life, just like bodily birth, which, though a unique event in its own right, extends and is connected with the age of the person who is born. For if the connection between a person and their birth is severed they surely die, since the power of their birth is what keeps them alive. This is exactly what happens in our second birth from water and the Spirit. After that second birth, the one who is born remains and continues in the life of the Spirit, while if faith is severed, the very impetus behind the person's life is severed as well, and they die. This is the reason why baptism must be considered a new beginning for a new life. It is a reality of salvation, and the reality of the death of sin, "Likewise you also, reckon yourselves to be dead indeed to sin, but alive to God in Christ Jesus our Lord." (Rom 6:11)

For in baptism we are essentially empty vessels that are subsequently filled with the gift of God. After baptism, we must believe in what we have received, preach it, confess it, give thanks for it, and adhere to it. This can be clearly seen in the incident of the baptism of the people of Israel in the Red Sea. The work itself is God's and is free of charge, but it is imperative that the people submit, obey, and respond to the work of God. In short, God works and the people respond. However, in reality the majority of the people did not respond to the miracle of God. Thus, neither the miracle itself, nor its power and efficacy, were enough to make them believe and be saved. They did not submit to it in faith but instead returned to their sins. We can see therefore that the miracle in itself is freely given, but in return, faith and action are necessary.

And what is baptism? It is the miracles of Christ in his death and Resurrection, as well as the forgiveness of our sins. These grant us a spiritual and organic enlightenment in his body and his covenant, and the grace of the new life. These supernatural and intangible miracles, these interior miracles that surpass all intellect, God has desired to transfer to all of us, one by one, in order for each person to taste of it individually in baptism in a private and mystical way. It would have been difficult for man to believe in this miracle before receiving it. However, once he has received it, and has tasted it, felt it, and lived it, if he denies it, this grace is taken from him, and all its gifts, enlightenment, and relation with Christ. Consequently, man becomes a traitor to the grace of baptism, a betrayer of Christ, a betrayer of the blood by which he was sanctified, and contemptuous of the Spirit of grace. Such a man is worse than an unbeliever and cannot be renewed.

Faith is demanded of all those who are baptized, or else the new life is withdrawn from them and they become spiritually dead, that is, eternally dead, and have no renewal in Christ.

7

With the Holy Spirit and Fire: The Birth of a Church

The second birth from above of water and the Spirit is a divine, heavenly act. The Scriptures, starting especially from Jesus' dialogue with Nicodemus, confirm this.

> Most assuredly, I say to you, unless one *is born of water and the Spirit*, he cannot enter the kingdom of God. (Jn 3:5)

> Do not marvel that I said to you, 'You must be *born from above*'. (Jn 3:7)

> According to his mercy he saved us, through the *washing of regeneration* and renewing of the Holy Spirit. (Titus 3:5)

The birth indicated in (Jn 3:7) is a spiritual birth, which we can see in the expression *born from above*.

> Who were born, not of blood, nor of the will of the flesh, nor of the will of man, but of God. (Jn 1:13)

> That which is born of the flesh is flesh, and that which is born of the Spirit is spirit. (Jn 3:6)

In other words, the second birth is from a divine source, *from above*, from the Holy Trinity, from the Father,[1] from the Son,[2] and from

---

[1] Cf. Jas 1:18 ; 1 Pet 1:3
[2] Cf. Jn 1:12

the Holy Spirit,[3] though it was most commonly attributed to the Spirit. For baptism is the instrument by which the Spirit accomplishes this second birth.

The washing with water in baptism refers to the forgiveness of sins, as can be seen in the following passages

> Just as Christ also loved the church and gave himself for her, that he might sanctify and cleanse her with the washing of water by the word. (Eph 5:25,26)

> And there are three that bear witness on earth: the Spirit, the water, and the blood; and these three agree as one. (I Jn 5:8)

> Repent, and let every one of you be baptized in the name of Jesus Christ *for the remission of sins*; and you shall receive the gift of the Holy Spirit. (Acts 2:38)

> And now why are you waiting? Arise and be baptized, and *wash away your sins*, calling on the name of the Lord. (Acts 22:16)

> And such were some of you. But you were *washed*, but you were sanctified, but you were justified in the name of the Lord Jesus and by the Spirit of our God. (I Cor 6:11)

In as much as the Holy Spirit is given to the person who is baptized for his spiritual regeneration and sanctification, the two, water and the Spirit, work together. Water is the medium through which the Spirit acts, and the Spirit is the inherent power at work. Together, they are the two elements of baptism, the visible and the active. This explanation can be seen in Paul's epistle to Titus, "Not by works of righteousness which we have done, but according to his mercy he saved us, through the washing of regeneration and renewing of the Holy Spirit." (Titus 3:5)

Water here is an important element, which works with faith and the Word to wash away sins through the power of the Holy Spirit. Paul's words to the people of Ephesus support this, "That he might

---

[3] Cf. Titus 3:5 above

sanctify and cleanse her with the washing of water by the word." (Eph 5:26) Paul also highlights the role of the Spirit in saying," But you were washed, but you were sanctified, but you were justified in the name of the Lord Jesus and by the Spirit of our God." (I Cor 6:11) Here we can see the work of baptism and the work of the Spirit together without any separation. Both work together for cleansing, sanctification, and justification.

Starting from the baptism of Christ as described by John the Baptist, and as witnessed later on the day of Pentecost, fire becomes an essential element as well, in addition to water. "He will baptize you with the Holy Spirit and with fire." (Mt 3:11) Fire here is mentioned in this abstract sense because it is a characteristic of the work of the Spirit, and not, as some may have thought when they heard these words, actual physical fire. Instead, it is judgment and severe admonition, which burns all sinners and those who depart from righteousness. For "the Spirit and fire" are one and the same, accomplishing the two complementary aspects of baptism, demolishing of transgressions through burning, as well as the building up of righteousness with a fiery energy. While the baptism of John washed with water, the baptism with the Spirit and fire washes by burning, and both are for purification. Together, water and fire accomplish this dual act of burning away the external bodily blemishes, and enlightening the internal gifts of the soul, which is a necessary step in the process of preparing the disciples of the Lord.

The descent of the Holy Spirit on the day of Pentecost was an accurate fulfillment of that which Christ prophesied. This descent was accompanied with the appearance of the Spirit, "And suddenly there came a sound from heaven, as of a rushing mighty wind, and it filled the whole house where they were sitting. Then there appeared to them divided tongues, as of fire, and one sat upon each of them. And they were all filled with the Holy Spirit, "(Acts 2:2-4) as well as the gift of the Holy Spirit, "and [they] began to speak with other tongues, as the Spirit gave them utterance." (Acts 2:4). The gifts of the Holy Spirit continue,

> And it shall come to pass in the last days, says God, that I will pour out of my Spirit on all flesh; your sons and your daughters shall prophesy, your men shall see visions, your old men shall dream dreams.

> And on my menservants and on my maidservants I will pour out my Spirit in those days; and they shall prophesy. (Acts 2:17, 18)
>
> Repent, and let every one of you be baptized in the name of Jesus Christ for the remission of sins; and you shall receive the gift of the Holy Spirit. (Acts 2:38)
>
> While Peter was still speaking these words, the Holy Spirit fell upon all those who heard the word. And those of the circumcision who believed were astonished, as many as came with Peter, because the gift of the Holy Spirit had been poured out on the gentiles also. (Acts 10:44, 45)
>
> Then I remembered the word of the Lord, how he said, 'John indeed baptized with water, but you shall be baptized with the Holy Spirit'. (Acts 11:16)

It can be noted here from Peter's reference to the prophecy of Joel that the Holy Spirit that descended on the day of Pentecost came in completely different manifestations than what was commonly known in the Old Testament, as well as with an entirely new and different power. It is clear from the descent of the Holy Spirit according to both prophecy and the reality in Pentecost that the Holy Spirit's work is far reaching and extends without boundaries or limitations. In the Old Testament, the Holy Spirit descended on specific people appointed by God for prophecy, while in Pentecost, the Spirit descended on all the disciples, gathered together as the Church, or on all flesh. While the descent of the Holy Spirit in the past was temporal, partial, and for a specific purpose, we see him here coming in fullness and accompanying man permanently and consistently.

In the gospel of Luke we find, "Behold, I send the promise of my Father upon you; but tarry in the city of Jerusalem until you are endued with power from on high," (Lk 24:49) and also in the gospel of John, "But when the helper comes, whom I shall send to you from the Father, the Spirit of truth who proceeds from the Father, he will testify of me," (Jn 15:26) and also in the gospel of John, "However, when he, the Spirit of truth, has come, he will guide you into all truth;

With the Holy Spirit and Fire: The Birth of a Church

for he will not speak on his own authority, but whatever he hears he will speak; and he will tell you things to come. He will glorify me, for he will take of what is mine and declare it to you." (Jn 16:13, 14) It is clear here that the Holy Spirit came to fulfill the work of the Messiah and proclaim it, as well as to proclaim and guide us to all righteousness, which means the gift of the Holy Spirit in all its fullness. It is also clear that Christ is the one who sent the Holy Spirit from the Father. According to this description, the Spirit descended to continue the work and mission of Christ.

By this we understand that the baptism of the Holy Spirit that occurred in the day of Pentecost is the historical beginning based on the birth of Christ, his life, death, Resurrection, and ascension. This baptism distinguishes the beginning of the new aeon in the kingdom of God, and it contains all historical movements and raises them to a spiritual level. The work of the Holy Spirit with the disciples began with their preaching of the gospel to the whole world.

The day of Pentecost marked the birth of the Church in visible existence. On that day, the disciples were entrusted with the responsibility of the message and apostleship in all the regions close to them. Through the descent of the Holy Spirit, they obtained the spirit of filial love and strong unity in the Spirit. According to the promise of the Lord, they were indeed strengthened by power from on high, which appeared clearly in the beginning of the life of the Church, in her conflict with the leaders of the Jews and their institutions, and in their testimony before kings and rulers. This power of the Church was also manifested through miracles and signs, which silenced her opponents.[4]

We also see in Paul's epistles how the Holy Spirit would sanctify entire congregations at once, making them faithful witnesses and steadfast in Christian conduct. St Paul was helped immensely by the gift of speaking in tongues, through which many nations were able to hear the gospel in their own language. In this way, the nations were served through the baptism of the Holy Spirit, which helped open the door for the message of the kingdom to spread.

If we pay close attention to the first time *the baptism of water* was mentioned on the day of Pentecost, we find it in the words of Peter

---

[4] Cf. Acts 3:2; 5:12

the apostle. Addressing those who have just received the Holy Spirit and were convicted in their hearts upon hearing Peter's sermon, he said to them, "Repent, and let every one of you be baptized in the name of Jesus Christ for the remission of sins; and you shall receive the gift of the Holy Spirit." (Acts 2:38) Here, we see the work of the Holy Spirit in their hearts, leading them to faith in Christ, a personal and internal work. As a result of that work, Peter asks for the gift of the Holy Spirit on their behalf.

What happened next is also important, "Then those who gladly received his word were baptized; and that day about three thousand souls were added to them. " (Acts 2:41) The baptism of the Holy Spirit is hereby completed with the baptism of water in the name of Jesus Christ for repentance and forgiveness of sins.

What happened on the day of Pentecost can be summarized in this way. Through preaching and hearing of the redemptive and salvific work of Christ, the heart starts to accept the message and believes. Then the Holy Spirit descends, leading the believer to the baptismal font to be baptized in the name of Christ. In this way, the person is reborn again for Christ, and is renewed by the Holy Spirit for the new creation.

In the book of Acts, Christ opened his dialogue about baptism by saying, "For John truly baptized with water, but you shall be baptized with the Holy Spirit not many days from now...But you shall receive power when the Holy Spirit has come upon you; and you shall be witnesses to me in Jerusalem, and in all Judea and Samaria, and to the end of the earth." (Acts 1:5, 8) This meant that the baptism of John would change to the baptism of the Holy Spirit, whom Christ received in the Jordan.

We see here a mystical relationship between the baptism of Christ and the day of Pentecost. The most obvious manifestation of this relationship is the physical manifestation of the descent of the Holy Spirit – in the form of a dove in the case of Christ, and in the form of tongues of fire in the case of the apostles. In this way, we see that by the end of Christ's earthly ministry, the apostles start their own ministries supported by the same Holy Spirit. We also see that the Holy Spirit, which was only an expectation and a hope for John the Baptist, has become a present reality through Christ's Resurrection and ascension. Thus, baptism with the Holy Spirit became an eschatological reality, made real in the fullness of time through the pouring out of the Holy Spirit from the Father according to the promise, and in the name of Christ.[5]

The Holy Spirit who descended on the apostles established the Church's missionary activity and preaching of Christ the Lord, according to his command. Therefore, all of the miracles and powers of the Holy Spirit aimed at advancing the gospel, fulfilling the promise to Joel the prophet concerning the expected hope in the fullness of time, and the pouring of the Holy Spirit on all men.

---

[5] Cf. Lk 24:49 ; Acts 1:4

PART TWO

Baptism in History and the Fathers

Fr Athanasius Al-Maqary

1
Symbols and Types

The word for *type* in Greek is τύπος, which is translated as *type*, or *model*. The place and function of types in the New Testament is different from the Old Testament. In the Old, it was an expression or a sign of what will occur in the future, a foreshadowing if you will, while in the New symbols and types are made manifest in the Church here and now.

For the rock which brought forth water in the Old Testament was a type of Christ and the power of life that came forth from him, "For they drank of that spiritual rock that followed them, and that rock was Christ," (I Cor 10:4), while in the New Testament, Christ himself says, "If anyone thirsts, let him come to me and drink." (Jn 7:37) In another example, the blood of the lamb in the Old Testament was a type of the blood of Christ that purifies from every sin, while in Christ the type is no longer needed, because Christ himself is the truth and the reality.

Another example is the manna, which came down from heaven in the Old Testament, and was a type of Christ the bread of life, who said concerning himself, "I am the living bread which came down from heaven. If anyone eats of this bread, he will live forever; and the bread that I shall give is my flesh, which I shall give for the life of the world," (Jn 6:51) "Take, eat, this is my body." (Mt 26:26) Also, the exodus of the children of Israel from Egypt and their crossing of the Red Sea was a type of the salvation through the baptism of the new covenant. The serpent raised on a pole in the Old Testament was a type of the cross in the New. Salvation from death for those that looked at the bronze serpent was a type of the eternal salvation of those who always focus their attention on the cross. Thus we see that types in the Old Testament point to a reality in the New, and once the type has fulfilled its purpose, it is no longer needed. Therefore, in

Christ all types cease and lose the purpose for which they existed. For he himself said, "I am the truth," (Jn 14:6) and being God, he alone is the ever-present reality.

A radical difference exists between a type and the reality it foreshadows. It is the same radical difference between the law of the Old Testament, and the grace of the New. It is the ontological difference between the lamb offered instead of Isaac, and the death and Resurrection of Christ, or between an inanimate rock and Christ himself, or between a piece of wood thrown into the water to turn it sweet and the cross of Christ, which transforms the bitterness of life to sweetness.

These examples show us that the spiritual grace that we obtain from the truth could not have been fulfilled by the type alone, until that type had been in fact fulfilled and revealed in Jesus Christ. A type expresses a reality that carries within itself a higher reality, one that is not present, for a type hides more than what it reveals. A type represents what it typifies without being it in reality, (as for example the lamb offered for Isaac is indeed a type of Christ, but not Christ himself ontologically); otherwise a type would no longer be a type. It is possible to mentally comprehend the object of the type, but it remains far away from our full grasp until it is fulfilled and manifested. Finally, a type is not revealed to everyone, but only to those granted by God, "by revelation he made known to me the mystery," (Eph 3:3) for a type is understood through faith not rational intellect, while the object of the type requires only this rational intellect to be perceived and comprehended.

On the other hand, symbols occupy a different place in sacramental understanding. The word for *symbol* in Greek is σύμβολον and is derived from the verb συμβάλλω, which is translated "to join, unite, or gather together", and more specifically, "to compare one's own opinion with facts, and so to interpret." Fr Alexander Schmemann says that the distinction between symbol and reality did not exist for the early Church Fathers or early tradition. On the contrary, for the fathers, the symbol *implied* the reality, expressed it, and was the mode in which and through which this reality appeared. Thus, the fathers' usage of the word *symbol* and its variants was not vague or inaccurate, but was fundamentally different from its use by later theologians, who do not seem to realize that this later mutation in its meaning is clearly a theological tragedy. This is because a symbol is not simply a means to understanding a reality, a teaching aid, but a means for *participation*. A symbol can indeed be a teaching aid, but it has become, in its entirety, knowledge.

The complete truth of a Church sacrament lies not in the sacrament itself, but in the specific object it points to, that which it reveals and makes manifest, which is precisely Christ and his Kingdom. For the institution of the Church, sacrament means that the symbol is pointed to Christ, is fulfilled in Christ, is completed and becomes a Church sacrament in the true sense. Unfortunately, post-patristic theology began to minimize and eventually abandoned the relationship between symbol and sacrament through a gradual reductionism of symbol. This reductionism restricted itself to an understanding of faith in terms of knowledge, or the possibility of the knowledge of God through rational and intellectual means, while the patristic understanding of knowledge is through life and participation.

A symbol by its very nature reveals *the other* and communicates it to us as *the other*. It reveals the possibility of seeing what is invisible as invisible, the knowledge of the unknowable as unknowable, and the presence of the future as future. The symbol is a means of knowledge of that which cannot be known otherwise, for knowledge here depends on participation – the living encounter with and entrance into that epiphany of reality, to which the symbol points the way. The symbol therefore is not only related to sacrament, but is its very source and a condition for its existence.

Symbol and reality have now become two mutually exclusive categories, two contrasting systems. Post-patristic theology has so denigrated the value of symbol to the point that symbol and reality have become not only different, but also opposed to one another. This mutation in post-patristic theology in the meaning of sacrament is manifested in its isolation of sacraments apart from their liturgical context, the so-called sacramental theology of the western variety. The worst mistake of post-patristic theology then lies in its separation of sacraments from the liturgy, since the liturgy is the complete expression of the life and faith of the Church. This separation is in reality a separation between the sacrament and the symbol. Thus, sacraments have become "means of grace", closed, existing in themselves, apart from any liturgical or spiritual context, and in no need for anything to secure its "validity" apart from the satisfaction of a

Symbols and Types

specific set of criteria. The liturgy was denied its specific function, which is to link the sacrament to its meaning.[1]

The Church sacraments, insofar as they unite us to Christ, are not types or figures to express the faith of the Church, or means to attain that faith, but rather the fulfillment of that faith. They are the faith itself, and not a representation of its meaning. The faith of the Church is, in its fullness, the obtaining of the life and mind of Christ, and therefore the obtaining of the life of the Church. These are the sacraments in which Christ has deposited his life to be communicated in turn to the Church, and from her to all those who believe in him. Not that the sacraments are means to an end, but the fountain of that end and its permanence. For separation from the sacraments is separation from the life of Christ, since our life in Christ is not fulfilled except through the sacraments, or indeed in them. In short, once the sacraments cease, the work of the Church ceases immediately, and by consequence, the life of Christ in us.

Many people have entered the Church through baptism, as a way to join the community of the Church, though they continue to live their lives in separation from the Church and the community. These did not live their lives from within the sacrament of baptism, since for them baptism was a past event, no longer relevant. The more advanced in years they became, the more separated they became from the Church. But what is our baptism except our constant partaking in the death and Resurrection of the Lord, death to the world, and life in the Lord? And what is our baptism except our rejection and renouncing of Satan, the world, its deception, and its evil? Our baptism is the *continuous* acceptance of Christ in our life, the living according to his commandments, and serving him in fear all the days of our life. Indeed, we proclaimed all of this on the day of our baptism, or rather our parents proclaimed this on our behalf until we came to understand what we proclaimed and received the faith of our fathers: "I profess You, O Christ my God, and all your saving laws, and all your quickening service, and all your life giving works."

Should the sacraments remain after all this mere symbols, signs, and means? This western scholastic understanding has crept into Orthodox theology and polluted our most precious possession; a faith, living and lived in the Church and her liturgy and sacraments, not a

---

[1] Adapted from Alexander Schmemann, *For the Life of the World: Sacraments and Orthodoxy*, 135-151.

rational faith that fills the mind but not the heart, and adds knowledge at the expense of virtue.

2

Baptism and the Holy Spirit: Types from Scripture

There are many types of baptism in the Old Testament, as well as references to the presence and role of the Holy Spirit. The fathers of the Church have written extensively about these types, explaining their meaning and how they were all fulfilled in the New Testament.

The Spirit's Presence in the Creation Narrative

Ambrose (339 – 397 AD) wrote,

> Consider, however, how ancient is the mystery prefigured even in the origin of the world itself. In the very beginning, when God made the heaven and the earth, 'the Spirit' it is said, 'moved upon the waters.' (Gen 1:2). He who was moving upon waters, was he not working upon the waters? But why should I say, 'working'? As regards his presence he was moving. Was he not working who was moving? Recognize that he was working in that making of the world, when the prophet says: 'By the word of the Lord were the heavens made, and all their strength by the spirit of his mouth.' (Ps 33:6) Each statement rests upon the testimony of the prophet, both that he was moving and that he was working. Moses says that he was moving, David testifies that he was working.[1]

---

[1] *On the Mysteries* III. 9 (NPNF-II 10:318).

Thus we see that creation itself came to be through water, the Spirit, and God's word, just as we too are born by water, the Spirit and God's word, as the Lord said, "Most assuredly I say to you, unless one is born of water and the Spirit, he cannot enter the kingdom of God," (Jn 3:5) as well as the apostle's saying, "having been born again, not of corruptible seed but incorruptible, through the word of God which lives and abides forever." (I Pet 1:23).

The Flood and Noah's Ark

As far as the flood and Noah's ark as a type of baptism in the New Testament, Ambrose wrote:

> Take another testimony. All flesh was corrupt by its iniquities. 'My Spirit,' says God, 'shall not remain among men, because they are flesh.' (Gen 6:3) Whereby God shows that the grace of the Spirit is turned away by carnal impurity and the pollution of grave sin. Upon which, God, willing to restore what was lacking, sent the flood and bade just Noah go up into the ark. And he, after having, as the flood was passing off, sent forth first a raven, which did not return, sent forth a dove which is said to have returned with an olive twig.[2] You see the water, you see the wood [of the ark], you see the dove, and do you hesitate as to the mystery?
>
> The water, then, is that in which the flesh is dipped, that all carnal sin may be washed away. All wickedness is there buried. The wood is that on which the Lord Jesus was fastened when he suffered for us. The dove is that in the form of which the Holy Spirit descended, as you have read in the New Testament, who inspires in you peace of soul and tranquility of mind. The raven is the figure of sin, which goes

---

[2] Cf. Gen 7:1

forth and does not return, if, in you, too, inwardly and outwardly righteousness be preserved.[3]

The Crossing of the Red Sea

The crossing of the Red Sea as a foreshadowing of the baptism of the New Testament occupies a prominent place in the writings of the Fathers. Aside from St Paul, the first of the Fathers to speak about the crossing of the Red Sea as a symbol of baptism was Clement of Alexandria (150 – 215 AD), followed by Origen (185 – 254 AD), who reveals the theological basis of this symbol, based on the writings of St Paul:

> Do you see how much Paul's teaching differs from the literal meaning? What the Jews supposed to be a crossing of the sea, Paul calls a baptism; what they supposed to be a cloud, Paul asserts is the Holy Spirit. He wishes that to be understood in a similar manner to this which the Lord taught in the Gospels, 'Unless a man be born again of water and the Holy Spirit, he cannot enter the kingdom of heaven.' (Jn 3:5)[4]

Origen continues later,

> What then are we taught by these words? We already mentioned above what the apostle's understanding is in these matters. He calls this 'baptism in Moses consummated in the cloud and in the sea' that you also who are baptized in Christ, in water and the Holy Spirit, might know that the Egyptians are following you and wish to recall you to their service. They are 'the rulers of this world,' of course, and 'the spiritual evils' which you previously served. These attempts to follow, but you descend in the water and come out unimpaired, the filth of sins having been

---

[3] On the Mysteries III 10
[4] *Homily V on Exodus*, The Fathers of the Church, Vol. 71, trans. Ronald Heine (Washington, DC: Catholic University Press, 1982), 276.

Baptism and the Holy Spirit: Types from Scripture

washed away. You ascend 'a new man' prepared to 'sing a new song.' But the Egyptians who follow you are drowned in the abyss.[5]

The scholar Tertullian (160 – 225 AD) confirms this:

> When the people, set unconditionally free, escaped the violence of the Egyptian king by crossing over *through water*, it was *water* that extinguished the king himself, with his entire forces. What figure more manifestly fulfilled in the sacrament of baptism? The nations are set free from the world by means of *water*, to wit: and the devil, their old tyrant, they leave quite behind, overwhelmed in the *water*.[6]

As for Didymus the Blind (313 – 398 AD), he mentions the crossing of the Red Sea as a type of baptism:

> The Red Sea receives the Israelites who did not doubt and delivered them from the perils of the Egyptians who pursued them: and so the whole history of the flight from Egypt is a type of the salvation obtained through baptism. Egypt represents the world, in which we harm ourselves if we live badly; the people are those who are now enlightened (baptized); the waters, which are for these people the means of salvation, represent baptism; Pharaoh and his soldiers are the devil and his satellites.[7]

Ambrose continues his discourse mentioned previously about the crossing of the Red Sea by the children of Israel as a third type of the baptism of water and the Spirit:

> There is also a third testimony, as the Apostle teaches us: 'For all our fathers were under the cloud, and all passed through the sea, and were all baptized to Moses in the cloud and in the sea.' (I Cor 10:1-2) And further, Moses himself says in his song: 'Thou

---

[5] Ibid.
[6] *On Baptism* IX (ANF 3:673).
[7] De Trinitate, II 14. Cited in Jean Danielou, *From Shadows to Reality: Studies in the Biblical Typology of the Fathers* (Westminster, MD: The Newman Press, 1960), 178.

sentest thy Spirit and the sea covered them.' (Ex 15:10) You observe that even then holy baptism was prefigured in that passage of the Hebrews wherein the Egyptian perished, the Hebrew escaped. For what else are we daily taught in this sacrament but that guilt is swallowed up and error done away, but that virtue and innocence remain unharmed?[8]

Basil the Great (330 – 379 AD) eloquently summarizes the meaning of the crossing of the Red Sea and says,

> If Israel had not crossed the sea, it would not have escaped from the Pharaoh; if you do not cross the water you will not be separated from the harsh tyranny of the devil. Israel would not have drunk of that spiritual rock if it were not baptized figuratively; nor would anyone give you true drink if you were not baptized. Israel ate of the bread of angels[9] after being baptized; how will you eat the living bread unless you have first received baptism?[10]

The Crossing of the Jordan

Origen is considered to have been the first to interpret the crossing of the Jordan as a type of baptism. Many Fathers after him borrowed the same idea, especially Gregory of Nyssa (330 – 395 AD), Basil the Great (330 – 379 AD), and John Chrysostom (347 – 407 AD). In a homily on the baptism of Christ, Gregory of Nyssa says,

> The people of the Hebrews, as we learn, after many sufferings, and after accomplishing their weary course in the desert, did not enter the land of promise until it had first been brought, with Joshua for its guide and the pilot of its life, to the passage of the Jordan. But it is clear that Joshua also, who set up the twelve stones in the stream, was anticipating the

---

[8] On the Mysteries III 12.
[9] Ps 77:25
[10] *Protreptic on Holy Baptism* 425. Cited in *Baptism: Ancient Liturgies and Patristic Texts* (ed. André Hamman. Staten Island, NY: Alba House, 1967), 78.

coming of the twelve disciples, the ministers of baptism.[11]

The Washing of Naaman the Syrian in the Jordan

Regarding this, Ambrose wrote:

> Lastly, let the lessons lately gone through from the kings teach you. Naaman was a Syrian, and suffered from leprosy, nor could he be cleansed by any. Then a maiden from among the captives said that there was a prophet in Israel, who could cleanse him from the defilement of the leprosy. And it is said that, having taken silver and gold, he went to the king of Israel. And he, when he heard the cause of his coming, rent his clothes, saying, that occasion was rather being sought against him, since things were asked of him which pertained not to the power of kings. Elisha, however, sent word to the king, that he should send the Syrian to him, that he might know there was a God in Israel. And when he had come, he bade him dip himself seven times in the river Jordan. Then he began to reason with himself that he had better waters in his own country, in which he had often bathed and never been cleansed of his leprosy; and so remembering this, he did not obey the command of the prophet, yet on the advice and persuasion of his servants he yielded and dipped himself. And being forthwith cleansed, he understood that it is not of the waters but of grace that a man is cleansed. Understand now who is that young maid among the captives. She is the congregation gathered out of the gentiles, that is, the Church of God held down of old by the captivity of sin, when as yet it possessed not the liberty of grace, by whose counsel that foolish people of the gentiles heard the word of prophecy as to which it had before been in doubt.

---

[11] On the Baptism of Christ (NPNF-II 5:522).

Afterwards, however, when they believed that it ought to be obeyed, they were washed from every defilement of sin. And he indeed doubted before he was healed; you are already healed, and therefore ought not to doubt.[12]

The Sacrifice of Elijah

Regarding this, Gregory of Nyssa wrote:

> Again, that marvelous sacrifice of the old Tishbite, that passes all human understanding, what else does it do but prefigure in action the faith in the Father, the Son, and the Holy Ghost, and redemption? For when all the people of the Hebrews had trodden underfoot the religion of their fathers, and fallen into the error of polytheism, and their king Ahab was deluded by idolatry, with Jezebel, of ill-omened name, as the wicked partner of his life, and the vile prompter of his impiety, the prophet, filled with the grace of the Spirit, coming to a meeting with Ahab, withstood the priests of Baal in a marvelous and wondrous contest in the sight of the king and all the people; and by proposing to them the task of sacrificing the bullock without fire, he displayed them in a ridiculous and wretched plight, vainly praying and crying aloud to gods that were not. At last, himself invoking his own and the true God, he accomplished the test proposed with further exaggerations and additions. For he did not simply by prayer bring down the fire from heaven upon the wood when it was dry, but exhorted and enjoined the attendants to bring abundance of water. And when he had thrice poured out the barrels upon the cleft wood, he kindled at his prayer the fire from out of the water, that by the contrariety of the elements, so concurring in friendly cooperation, he might show with

---

[12] On the Mysteries III 16

superabundant force the power of his own God. Now herein, by that wondrous sacrifice, Elijah clearly proclaimed to us the sacramental rite of baptism that should afterwards be instituted. For the fire was kindled by water thrice poured upon it, so that it is clearly shown that where the mystic water is, there is the kindling, warm, and fiery Spirit, that burns up the ungodly, and illuminates the faithful.[13]

The Circumcision of the Law

Circumcision remains one of the most prominent symbols of baptism, or rather more important than these other symbols. This is because it is a personal symbol, performed on man himself as a sign of a permanent covenant between him and God. Circumcision was the seal of the covenant between God on one hand and Abraham and his children on the other, and according to scriptural tradition it was required of every Hebrew boy on the eighth day.[14]

Sometimes, the meaning of circumcision was moral or ethical, as a symbol of humbling the pride of man. Other times, it was understood in terms of man's indebtedness to God, which circumcision repaid in part. Nonetheless, the central meaning of circumcision remains that of a covenant with God.

In addition, the fact that circumcision was performed on a child on the eighth day shows that his entrance into this covenant with God does not depend on his own voluntary participation. Rather, it is mainly divine providence that the child was born to parents from the people of God. Thus, circumcision becomes the covenant through which God chooses this child to become a member of his people, even before this child is able to comprehend this choice and calling.

However, once this child reached the proper age, this circumcision that he received as a distinguishing sign became a source of responsibility and commitment towards a set of duties that correspond to the privilege of belonging to the people of God. Thus, circumcision reveals that God's election came before man's assent, indeed,

---

[13] On the Baptism of Christ, 522
[14] Cf. Gen 17

before any possibility of such assent. God's calling came first, followed by man's response.

Circumcision also – though it only applies to males – reflects, albeit outwardly, the lower status of women in the Old Testament. The relationship of the woman to God, as members of his chosen people, was always through man, whether her father, husband, or brother, since the covenant was only with them, insofar as they were the ones carrying its visible sign.[15]

Even though circumcision is a visible bodily sign, it also carried a spiritual meaning in the Old Testament. Moses the prophet addresses the people and says, "The Lord delighted only in your fathers, to love them; and he chose their descendants after them, you above all peoples, as it is this day. Therefore circumcise the foreskin of your heart, and be stiff-necked no longer." (Deut 10:15-16) Thus, Stephen was correct when he admonished the Jews saying, "You stiff-necked and uncircumcised in heart and ears!" (Acts 7:51)

In the New Testament, St Paul marks a profound shift in the understanding of circumcision as a sign of the covenant between God and his people. Through this shift, St Paul renders circumcision irrelevant through its replacement by baptism. This can be clearly seen in his address to the Jews that accepted Christ, yet maintained circumcision in its ancient form. St Paul writes, "Therefore, if an uncircumcised man keeps the righteous requirements of the law, will not his uncircumcision be counted as circumcision? And will not the physically uncircumcised, if he fulfills the law, judge you who, even with your written code and circumcision, are a transgressor of the law? For he is not a Jew who is one outwardly, nor is circumcision that which is outward in the flesh; but he is a Jew who is one inwardly; and circumcision is that of the heart, in the Spirit, not in the letter; whose praise is not from men but from God." (Rom 2:26-29)

In another occasion, St Paul summarizes this previous idea and writes, "Circumcision is nothing and uncircumcision is nothing, but keeping the commandments of God is what matters." (I Cor 7:19) Finally, St Paul deals the final blow and writes, "Indeed I, Paul, say to you that if you become circumcised, Christ will profit you nothing. For in Christ Jesus neither circumcision nor uncircumcision avails anything, but faith working through love," (Gal 5:2,6)

---

[15] John Heron, *Christian Initiation*, Studia Liturgica, vol. 1, p. 33-34.

Circumcision has become irrelevant as an old covenant between God and his people, having been replaced with a new covenant, when Christ accepted it in himself, fulfilling the judgment of the law on behalf of all humanity. "In him you were also circumcised with the circumcision made without hands, by putting off the body of the sins of the flesh, by the circumcision of Christ, buried with him in baptism, in which you also were raised with him through faith in the working of God, who raised him from the dead." (Col 2:11-12)

Circumcision therefore was the most prominent type of baptism in the Old Testament. Though its understanding as a covenant remained in the Jewish background upon which Christian sacraments were based, circumcision was ultimately superseded by the spiritual circumcision of baptism.

The Pool of Bethesda

The scholar Tertullian was the first to point to the pool of Bethesda as a symbol of baptism. Tertullian wrote regarding the healing of the man at the pool of Bethesda:

> If it seems a novelty for an angel to be present in waters, an example of what was to come to pass has forerun. An angel, by his intervention, was wont to stir the pool at Bethesda. They who were complaining of ill health used to watch for him; for whoever had been the first to descend into them, after his washing, ceased to complain. This figure of corporeal healing sang of a spiritual healing, according to the rule by which things carnal are always antecedent.[1]

In addition, Ambrose wrote:

> Therefore it is said: 'An angel of the Lord went down according to the season into the pool, and the water was troubled; and he who first after the troubling of the water went down into the pool was healed of whatsoever disease he was held.' (Jn 5:4) This pool was at Jerusalem, in which one was healed

---

[1] On Baptism V, 673.

every year, but no one was healed before the angel had descended. Because of those who believed not the water was troubled as a sign that the angel had descended. They had a sign, you have faith; for them an angel descended, for you the Holy Spirit; for them the creature was troubled, for you Christ himself, the Lord of the creature, works. Then one was healed, now all are made whole; or more exactly, the Christian people alone, for in some even the water is deceitful. The baptism of unbelievers heals not but pollutes. The Jew washes pots and cups, as though things without sense were capable of guilt or grace. But do you wash this living cup of yours, that in it your good works may shine and the glory of your grace be bright. For that pool was as a type, that you might believe that the power of God descends upon this font.[2]

Didymus the Blind also agreed when he wrote:

> We should find out, in the presence of those by whom it is mentioned, that the pool which is in Jerusalem, whose name in Hebrew is Bethesda, is known to be an image of baptism, though it does not happen to be the truth itself. For the image is only for a time, whereas the truth is decidedly eternal. For this reason, only once a year was the water moved by the angel, and only one person, the first that descends into the water, was healed, and even then only from the diseases of the flesh, not of the soul. On the other hand, real baptism, which was instituted after the appearance of the Son of God and the descent of the Holy Spirit, happens every day, or rather every hour. Truly then, all those who descend are constantly rendered eternally free from all sins.[3]

---

[2] On the Mysteries IV
[3] *De Trinitate* 2 (PG 39:705). Since translations of this work that is attributed to Didymus are not accessible in English, I decided to translate this passage myself, not relying on the Arabic quote as found in Fr Athanasius' work. The original Greek text

In addition, John Chrysostom also spoke about Bethesda in homily 36 on the Gospel of St John, as well as Gregory of Nazianzus (329 – 389 AD) in his oration on holy baptism.

The Healing of the Man Born Blind

For many centuries, the Coptic Church has performed baptisms most often on the Lenten Sunday called *The Sunday of the Man Born Blind*. This Sunday is still commonly called *the Sunday of Baptism*, because of the strong connection between this miracle and the sacrament of baptism. Cyril of Alexandria spoke about this and wrote:

> Accepting the cure wrought upon this blind man as a type of the calling of the gentiles, we will again tell the meaning of the mystery, summing it up in few words. First then because it was merely in passing, and after leaving the Jewish temple, that he saw the blind man: and again from this circumstance also, that without entreaty and no man soliciting him, but rather of his own accord and from a spontaneous inclination, the Savior came to a determination to heal the man; hence we shall profitably look upon the miracle as symbolical. It shows that as no entreaty has been made by the multitude of the gentiles, for they were all in error, God, being indeed in his nature good, of his own will has come forward to show mercy unto them...
>
> On the Sabbath too was the work of healing accomplished, the Sabbath being capable thereby completely to exhibit to us a type of the last age of the

---

is presented here: Εὕροιμεν δὲ ἂν πρὸς τοῖς μνημονευθεῖσι καὶ τὴν κολυμβήθραν τὴν ἐν Ἰερουσαλὴμ, ᾗ ὄνομα Ἑβραϊστὶ Βηθεσδὰ, ὁμολογουμένως εἰκόνα τοῦ βαπτίσματος, ἀλλ'οὐκ αὐτὴν τυγχάνουσαν τὴν ἀλήθειαν· ἡ γὰρ εἰκὼν πρὸς καιρὸν, ἡ δὲ ἀλήθεια εἰς αἰωνιότητα κρίνεται. Διὸ καὶ ἅπαξ τοῦ ἐνιαυτοῦ ὑπὸ ἀγγέλου κινηθὲν τὸ ἐν αὐτῇ ὕδωρ, καὶ ἕνα μόνον τὸν πρῶτον κατιόντα, καὶ σωματικὸν πάθος, οὐχὶ δὲ καὶ ψυχικὸν ἐθεράπευεν Τὸ γὰρ αὐθεντικὸν βάπτισμα, μετὰ τὴν τοῦ Υἱοῦ καὶ τοῦ ἁγίου Πνεύματος ἐπιφάνειαν, καὶ καθ' ἑκάστην ἡμέραν, μᾶλλον δὲ ὥραν· ἀληθέστερον δὲ, ἀδιαλείπτως καὶ πάντας τοὺς κατιόντας, καὶ ἀπὸ πάσης ἁμαρτίας αἰωνίως ἐλευθεροῖ·

present world, in which the Savior has made light to shine on the gentiles. For the Sabbath is the end of the week, and the Only Begotten took up His abode and was manifested to us all in the last time, and in the concluding ages of the world...

For by anointing with the clay he makes good that which is (so to speak) lacking or vitiated in the nature of the eye, and thus shows that he is the one who formed us in the beginning, the Creator and Fashioner of the universe...

And the power of the action possesses a sort of mystical significance; for that which we said just now with reference to this, and what we consider may be understood by it, we will mention again. It was not otherwise possible for the gentiles to thrust off the blindness which affected them, and to behold the Divine and holy light, that is, to receive the knowledge of the Holy and Consubstantial Trinity, except by being made partakers of his Holy body, and washing away their gloom-producing sin, and renouncing the authority of the devil, namely in holy baptism...

We by faith are washed, not for the putting away of the filth of the flesh, as it is written,[4] but as it were washing away a sort of defilement and uncleanness of the eyes of the understanding, in order that in the future, being purified, we may be able in pureness to behold the Divine beauty.[5]

---

[4] Cf. 1 Pet 3:21
[5] Commentary on the Gospel According to John VI

3

The Time of Baptism

In the early years of Christianity, baptism was administered on the eve of Pascha, since a strong connection existed between the baptismal rite and the celebration of Pascha since at least the 3rd century, as mentioned by Origen in a Paschal oration that has been discovered recently.[1] Soon thereafter, the feast of Pentecost also became an occasion suitable for administering baptism, followed by the feast of Theophany. Regarding the first two feasts, Pascha and Pentecost, the scholar Tertullian wrote:

> The Passover affords a more than usually solemn day for baptism; when, withal, the Lord's passion, in which we are baptized, was completed. After that, Pentecost is a most joyous space for conferring baptisms; wherein, too, the resurrection of the Lord was repeatedly proved among the disciples.[2]

Indeed, the Syriac Orthodox Church preserved the custom of administering baptism on Pascha, as witnessed by *The Testament of the Lord*, Aphrahat (early 4th century), and Cyril of Jerusalem (315-368).[3] In addition, Gregory of Nazianzus addresses those who postpone baptism pointing to the feast of Theophany as another opportunity for baptism, saying:

> You rely upon this or that, and 'pretend pretences in sins;' (Ps 41:4) I am waiting for Epiphany; I prefer Easter; I will wait for Pentecost.[4]

Similarly, the church of Jerusalem, as well as the Armenian Church, preserved the tradition of administering baptism on any of these three

---

[1] Annick Martin, Athanase d'Alexandrie et l'Eglise d'Egypte au IVe siècle (328-373), (Rome, 1996), 166.
[2] *On Baptism* XIX (ANF 3:678)
[3] Fernand Cabrol & R.P. dom Henri Leclercq, *Dictionnaire d'Archeologie Chretienne et de Liturgie* (DACL)(Paris, 1925), 276.
[4] *Oration on Holy Baptism* XXIV (NPNF-II 7:368)

feasts.⁵ As far as the church of Alexandria, early manuscripts show that baptisms were performed on the feasts of Pascha and Pentecost only, while in some other eastern churches – according to the testimony of Socrates⁶ – baptisms were performed only on Theophany. Nonetheless, the eve of Pascha remained the most prominent baptismal season in the early Church, preceded as it was by the Lenten season, which was a suitable period to instruct the catechumens in the basic tenets of the Christian faith before their baptism. Regarding this last point, John Chrysostom writes:

> I was seeking to tell you why our fathers passed by all the other seasons of the year and ordained that your souls be initiated during this season, and I said that observance of the time was not a simple or random thing. For it is always the same grace and it is not hindered by the season, for the grace is from God...Why did our fathers ordain this feast at this time? Our king has now conquered in the war against the barbarians. And all the demons are barbarians, and more savage than barbarians. Now he has destroyed sin, now he has put down death and has subjected the devil, he has taken his captives.
>
> And so it is that on this day we celebrate the memory of those victories, and on this account our fathers ordained that the king's gifts be distributed at this time, for this is the custom of conquerors...Our fathers also ordained this celebration in order that you might also be the master's partner throughout the season. St Paul says, he was crucified on the wood. Be crucified yourself through your baptism. For, he says, baptism is a cross and a death.⁷

---

⁵ DACL, 295.

⁶ Socrates V, 22. (NPNF-II 2). Though I was unable to find any references to this in Socrates' *Ecclesiastical History*, the theory that Baptisms were administered on Theophany in many places, particularly East Syria, is well attested. Cf. Maxwell Johnson, *The Christian Rites of Initiation: Their Evolution and Interpretation* (Collegeville, MN 2007). (Ed. Note)

⁷ The Eleventh Instruction, 1. Cited in St. John Chrysostom Baptismal Instructions (Westminster, 1963), 150.

Furthermore, John Chrysostom identifies the exact time of baptism as midnight on the eve of Pascha, that is, immediately before the Paschal Eucharistic service. In another passage, Chrysostom expresses the wonderful joy of the Church with her new members:

> After two days the bridegroom is coming. Arise, kindle your lamps, and by their shining light receive you the king of heaven. Arise and keep watch. For not during the day but in the middle of the night the bridegroom comes to you. This is the custom for the bridal procession – to give over the brides to the bridegrooms late in the evening.[8]

In Egypt, the exact time of baptism, the moment of immersion, was at the morning of Pascha at cockcrow. In Syria and Palestine, baptisms were administered at the beginning of the Paschal vigil, which starts at sunset on Saturday. This is mentioned by Jacques Goar in his Syriac Euchologion published in 1647, in which is written, "Beginning at sunset, candidates for baptism are baptized after one reading."[9] Similarly, in an address to the newly baptized, Cyril of Jerusalem says, "know the effect wrought upon you on that evening of your baptism."[10]

The eve of Pascha is the dividing line between the two most solemn events in the life of the Church, the burial of the Lord and his rising again after three days, victorious over death. Thus, the thrice immersion in water also became a sign of following in the footsteps of Christ, through death, burial, and rising again with him.[11] The eve of Pascha is truly the most special and solemn eve in the Church's calendar, as Augustine calls it. What a heavenly night, filled with hymns of joy and gladness, while the joy of Pascha is mingled with joy over the souls that were newly added to the body of Christ. Indeed, the joy felt by those newly baptized was reciprocated by the joy of the faithful, who spent the season of Lent supporting those catechumens with their prayers and supplications on their behalf, so that

---

[8] Ibid., 161.
[9] To my knowledge, Jacques Goar published a Constantinopolitan Euchologion, not a Syriac one. The quote above is a direct translation of Fr Athanasius' undocumented reference. (Ed. Note)
[10] Lecture XIX: First Lecture on the Mysteries 1 (NPNF-II, 7:144).
[11] Cf. Archimandrite Hananiah Kassab, *Majmu'at Al-Shar' Al-kanasy*, (Manshurat Al-nur, 1975), 231

THE BIRTH FROM ON HIGH

they may be worthy to receive this great mystery, the mystery of the birth from above, the mystery of salvation, deliverance and resurrection.

The custom of administering baptisms on the eve of Pascha remained in existence until the 12th century, since we find references to baptism at that time until the 12th century in both east and west. However, these references start to show up less often beginning with the 9th century, and ultimately disappear by the 12th.[12] Going back to the Alexandrian tradition, we find that, while baptism itself was administered on the eve of Pascha, the beginning of the rite started immediately after the conclusion of the Great Friday prayers. We have evidence for this from a story mentioned in *The History of the Coptic Patriarchs* of Sawirus ibn Al-Muqaffa'. An Antiochian woman crossed the sea to baptize her child in Alexandria by Pope Peter of Alexandria the seal of martyrs.[13] After experiencing many unforeseen circumstances in the middle of the sea she arrived at Alexandria, where the Latin text of the story mentions the following important note, "And after the great day of preparation, which is the sixth Friday of the forty day fast, when baptisms are usually administered to infants..."[14] However, the term preparation, *parasceves*, which is the original name for Good Friday, did not appear in the translation done by B.T.A Evetts of *The History*, where it says instead, "So when they entered the city by the help of the merciful God, since that day was in the week of Baptism, which is the sixth week of the fast,[15] when infants are baptized... And he gave to the two children of the holy mysteries. And he took them and their mother into his house until they had kept the

---

[12] *Majalat Al-nur*, issue 6 (Lebanon, 1985).
[13] Both *BN Arabe 100*, and *Vatican Copt 44* in the Vatican library claim that it was Pope Theophilus the 23rd patriarch of Alexandria. Cf. A. van Lantchoot, "Le Ms. Vatic. Copte 44 et le livre de Chreme (MSS. Paris arabe 100)," *Le Museon*, 45, books 3-4, (1932): 5-6.
[14] ipso die parasceves Dominicae sextae je junii quadragesimalis quo in fantibus baptismus administrabatur...
[15] The phrase "the sixth week of the fast" together with "the sixth Friday of the forty day fast" in the Latin text is an added interpolation by the copyist and cannot be in the original. All the documents known to us thus far testify that the forty-day fast became known in the church of Alexandria in the days of Athanasius (328-373), and what Origen mentioned regarding this fast in his commentary on Leviticus is most likely an interpolation by Rufinus, who translated the works of Origen to Latin. At any rate, whether the forty-day fast became known in Alexandria in the days of Athanasius or before him, it was he who canonized it.

feast of the holy Easter. Then they returned to their own city in peace."[16]

Similarly, Johann Vansleb, the Dominican monk who visited Egypt in the 17th century, testified to the same custom based on the testimony of Macarius bishop of Memphis,[17] who lived during the time of Pope Cosmas III (AD 920-932). Nonetheless, A. Butler denies the testimony attributed to Bishop Macarius, casting doubts on its authenticity,[18] though other historians and scholars regard it as further proof for the authenticity of the story mentioned in *The History of the Coptic Patriarchs.*[19]

As far as the Constantinopolitan rite, the *Barberini Codex* of the 8th century has preserved for us the custom at Constantinople regarding the appropriate baptismal season. It is titled, "The renunciation and adherence which takes place Holy Friday of the Pasch, with the archbishop presiding, and all the catechumens assembled in the very holy church."[20] Similarly, a Greek euchologion from Sinai from the 11th century offers another proof for this ancient Alexandrian tradition, in which the title given for the rite of renouncing Satan is: Ἀπόταξις καὶ σύνταξις γενομένη ὑπο τοῦ ἀρχιεπισκόπου τῇ ἁγίᾳ παρασκευῇ τοῦ πάσχα [The renouncing and the adherence to Christ that are done by the archbishop on the holy day of preparation of Pascha.] What is meant here are the rituals of preparing the catechumens, not the actual rites of immersion. These rites of preparation are followed the next day with the Paschal vigil itself, in which the rite of baptism is accomplished. Thus, we see here the Alexandrian tradition confirmed by Greek manuscripts as well.

These ancient documents take us back to a time when the process of preparing the catechumens was still an important and practical process, since baptism of adults was still the norm. This Greek euchologion reveals a distinctive teaching to the catechumens, where they are presented with the dual covenant that they are about to declare and

---

[16] B.T.A. Evetts, The History of the Patriarchs of the Coptic Church of Alexandria, Arabic Text Edited, Translated and Annotated, PO 10 (Paris, 1912), 387.
[17] This story was in fact not mentioned by Macarius, Bishop of Memphis in the 10th cent., as Vansleb claims, but occurred in an epistle by another bishop from the 12th cent. The text of both epistles can be found in *BN Arabe 100*, and *Vatican Copt 44*.
[18] A.J. Butler, *The Ancient Coptic Churches of Egypt*, vol. II (Oxford, 1884), 264.
[19] DACL, 258
[20] Thomas Finn, The Liturgy of Baptism in the Baptismal Instructions of St John Chrysostom, (Washington, DC 1967), 114

adhere to; the renouncing of Satan and all his angels and the confession of Christ and all his life-giving commandments. This is precisely what we find in *The Apostolic Constitutions* VII, "And when it remains that the catechumen is to be baptized, let him learn what concerns the renunciation of the devil, and the joining himself with Christ."[21] This renunciation and adherence were followed by certain litanies and a short prayer, but the current rite, added much later to accommodate infant baptism, only retains the formulas of renunciation and adherence and a concluding prayer, eliminating some of its more ancient elements.[22] Clearly, the final preparations for baptism started on Good Friday. Given the large number of candidates for baptism, it was surely impractical to perform all the rites in a single day, and for this reason, we find that the actual act of immersion in water was moved to Bright Saturday, and immediately before the beginning of the Paschal service.

Similarly, the Coptic *Canons of the Apostles* refers to the same final stages before immersion, which were performed on Bright Saturday. "And when the day approaches in which they shall be baptized, let the bishop exorcise each one of them, that he may know that they are pure."[23] Later in the 11th century, as the numbers of candidates for baptism declined, we see that the actual rite of baptism had begun to be performed on Good Friday. Since the canons of Pope Christodoulos (AD 1047-1077) prohibit baptisms during Holy Week and the period of Pentencost, we can deduce that at his time, this practice occurred often enough to merit a canon prohibiting it.

Alternatively, the church of Alexandria often administered baptisms on the eve of Theophany, at the occasion of the baptism of Christ.[24] Likewise, the feast of Theophany occupied a special place in terms of administering baptisms in Edessa, as evidenced by the hymns of Ephraim the Syrian that are chanted on that feast.[25] One however should not lose sight of the fact that the Church ultimately administered baptisms any time it was needed. Regarding this, Basil of Caesarea wrote,

---

[21] The Apostolic Constitutions VII:40 (ANF 7:476)
[22] DACL, 290
[23] Henry Tattam, The Apostolical Constitutions or The Canons of the Apostles in Coptic with an English Translation, (London, 1848), 52
[24] Coptic Encyclopedia, 338
[25] DACL, 276

> There is different season for everything. A season for sleep, and a season for watchfulness; A season for war, and a season for peace. But all of man's life is a season for baptism! For neither are living bodies able to subsist, nor are souls capable of coming together unto existence, without knowing the creator.[26]

Similarly, the scholar Tertullian himself, who earlier told us about the appropriate seasons for baptisms, also writes in the same treatise, "However, every day is the Lord's; every hour, every time, is apt for baptism. If there is a difference in the solemnity, distinction there is none in the grace."[27] In addition, the canons of Pope Gabriel V (AD 1409-1427) allow for baptisms at any time, for it says, "If they bring to you an infant to be baptized before the mother is purified, baptize the infant immediately, though he may be a day old."[28]

Later, in the latter half of the 10th century, the Sunday before the Lord's entry into Jerusalem, known as The Sunday of the Man Born Blind, or The Sunday of Baptism, became reserved for baptisms. This is so, not only in the Coptic Church, but also in many eastern churches. A homily by Cyril of Alexandria on the Gospel of John cited earlier shows the connection between opening the eyes of the man born blind and baptism.

---

[26] Καιρὸς μὲν οὖν ἄλλοις ἄλλος ἐπιτήδειος. ἴδιος ὕπνου, καὶ ἴδιος ἐγρηγόρσεως. ἴδιος πολέμου, καὶ ἴδιος εἰρήνης. καιρὸς δὲ βαπτίσματος ἅπας ὁ τῶν ἀνθρώπων βίος. Οὔτε γὰρ σώματι ζῆν μὴ ἀναπνέοντι δυνατόν, οὔτε ψυχῇ συνεστάναι, μὴ γνωριζούσῃ τὸν κτίσαντα. *Homilia exhortatoria ad sanctum baptisma*, (PG 31, 424-444).
[27] *Oration on Holy Baptism* XXIV (NPNF-II 7:368)
[28] Abdallah, A. L'Ordinamento Liturgico di Gabriele V 88 Patriarcho Copto (1409-27). (Cairo, 1962), 19.

4

The Catechumenate

The rank of the catechumens were those who attended services for the purpose of receiving instruction, and ultimately to qualify to join the body of Christ, through acceptance of the grace of baptism. Candidates for baptism, or the illuminated as they are often called, stood at the highest rank of the catechumens. Those were the ones ready to receive baptism, after having passed through various stages of catechetical instruction. Traditionally, catechumens were restricted to the narthex, the western area of the church, separated from the nave by a wooden screen. In the northern side of the narthex stood the baptistery, as mentioned in the *Arabic Didascalia*, "On the northwestern side, wherein is located the baptistery, there ought to be an isolated place in the church, where catechumens can find their place to listen to the holy books, the psalms, and the spiritual praises that are said in church."[1]

Not all catechumens were of pagan origin. There were in fact three types of catechumens in the early church. First, there were catechumens of Jewish background, who were given lessons from the Old Testament prophets and their fulfillment in the New Testament. Second, catechumens from gentile background, who were given lessons in accordance with their specific gentile background, which could explain why some fathers of the early church dedicated many of their writings to preaching Christianity based on pagan philosophy. Finally, there were catechumens who were children of Christian parents, who were largely the responsibility of their parents and godfathers. With the exception of those who were young, catechumens usually remained under the Church's guidance and instruction for two or three years, moving slowly from one rank to another within the catechumenate. Finally, baptism was only granted after the Church has been assured of the purity of their motives, their seriousness in

---

[1] William Soliman Qelada, *Aldisqolia-Taalim Alrosol*, (Cairo, 1979), ch. 35. Note that this particular chapter, as well as a few others, do not appear in the text of *The Apostolic Constitutions*, of which the *Arabic Didascalia* is supposed to be a translation.

seeking salvation, their steadfastness in the faith, and their acceptance to carry the cross and follow Christ.

Ranks of Penitents

The Mourners and Weepers: This rank stood outside the gates of the church, and was not allowed to attend the prayers. Gregory Thaumaturgus said in this regard, "Weeping takes place without the gate of the oratory; and the offender standing there ought to implore the faithful as they enter to offer up prayer on his behalf."[2] These mourners and lamenters made up the first rank of the penitents. It must have been quite a sight to behold, as believers made their way to the church for prayers, passing by those people mourning and lamenting, entreating them to pray for them. Indeed, the early Church possessed such warmth of spirit, and was a place for prayer and prayer only.

The Hearers: These made up the second rank of the penitents, and were allowed to pass through the main gates of the church – the original Royal Doors – and stood in the narthex. They were permitted to listen to the scriptural lessons (the epistles and gospel), the sermon, and they were dismissed immediately after the sermon. In the *Apostolic Constitutions*, we read, "and when he has ended his word of doctrine all standing up, let the deacon ascend upon some high seat, and proclaim, Let none of the hearers, let none of the unbelievers stay."[3] Thus, though they were allowed to attend the Liturgy of the Word, they were not allowed to attend the Eucharistic prayers.

The Kneelers: These stood in the very back of the church's nave, by the wooden screen separating the nave from the narthex. They were called kneelers because, not only were they allowed to hear the scriptural lessons, but also to attend certain litanies that were prayed on their behalf following the sermon. Before leaving the church, they would prostrate to the ground, receiving a blessing from the bishop. This blessing was called the prayer of the laying on of hands.

The 5th canon of the local council of Neocaesarea (AD 315) described this class as *kneelers*, while canon 19 of the provincial synod of Laodicea (AD 343) calls them the *those who are under penance*, "and after the catechumens have gone out, the prayer for those who are under penance; and, after these have passed under the hand of the

---

[2] *Canonical Epistle*, Canon xi (ANF 6:20).
[3] The Apostolic Constitutions, VIII:2 (ANF 7:483)

Bishop and departed, there should then be offered the three prayers of the faithful."[4] Finally, canon 14 of the first Ecumenical Council of Nicaea (AD 325) states, "Concerning catechumens who have lapsed, the holy and great Synod has decreed that, after they have passed three years only as hearers, they shall pray with the catechumens."[5] From this we see that the catechumens are in fact the penitents, who were allowed to attend the prayers of the catechumens, while those called hearers were not numbered among the catechumenate.

Candidates for Baptism: These were the last and highest rank of catechumens, and were also known in the east as the illuminated, while in the west they are called the elect or the chosen. These were selected from among the kneelers in the beginning of the Lenten fast in order to be prepared throughout the fast through instruction and receiving of the faith, in preparation for receiving baptism on the eve of pascha. Though there was no specific place for them in church, they usually stood with the kneelers.

From *The Apostolic Tradition of Hippolytus*, which was written ca. AD 215 and is considered the oldest church order after the *Didache*, we learn many aspects of the liturgical life of the universal church, especially the church of Alexandria, in which this particular document gained prominence. This document mentions the following in regards to selecting catechumens for baptism, "And when they have chosen those appointed to receive baptism, and have investigated their life, if they have lived in chastity, being catechumens; if they have honored the widows, if they have visited the sick, if they have fulfilled every good work."[6] After this process of selection, the names of those chosen were recorded in the church's books. However, the season of the year that was customary for this was not the same in all places. In Jerusalem, the recording of names used to occur on the first Sunday of Lent,[7] while in North Africa, this usually occurred on the fourth Sunday of Lent[8] and in the Assyrian church on Monday of the third week of Lent.[9] At variance with all of these is canon 45 of the local

---

[4] *Synod of Laodicea*, Canon XIX (NPNF-II 14:136)
[5] *The First Council of Nicaea*, Canon XIV (NPNF-II 14:31)
[6] Tattam, 52.
[7] John Wilkinson, *Egeria's Travels*. (Oxford, 2006), 161
[8] Augustine, Homily 217. As of the writing of this translation, I was unable to verify this particular reference (Ed. Note)
[9] Anton Baumstark, *Comparative Liturgy*, (London, 1958), 191

council of Laodicea (AD 364), which states, "Candidates for baptism are not to be received after the second week in Lent."[10]

After their official enrollment in the ranks of the catechumens, those illuminated as they were called spent their period of candidacy in fasting, vigils, and spiritual reading. Regarding the exact readings they were assigned, we find a reference to this in the 39th Festal Letter of Athanasius. After listing the rest of the Old Testament canon, he singles out The Wisdom of Solomon, The Wisdom of Sirach, Esther, Judith, and Tobit as especially beneficial for those who have newly joined the Church.[11]

The important liturgical fact that must be emphasized is that the scriptural lessons that were appointed for the Coptic daily lectionary during the Lenten fast, and especially those closer to Holy Week, were set in place specifically as instruction for the catechumens, before they were ever part of Eucharistic celebration. In fact, these scriptural lessons and readings (the prophecies, epistles, and gospel readings) that form the Lenten lectionary from Monday to Friday were known in the early Church before the development of daily Eucharistic celebration during Lent. Instead, these readings were read in the context of morning and evening services, otherwise known as the Synaxis, which did not include the offering of the Eucharist. Similarly, the old *Armenian Lectionary*, as well as the *Gregorian Kanonarion*, specify readings for the instruction of catechumens starting three weeks before Pascha. These readings consisted of Old Testament prophecies and selections from the epistles of St Paul, to be read from Monday to Friday on the weeks.[12]

Similarly, in the Assyrian church in the 10th century, according to the homilies attributed to George of Arbela, certain scriptural lessons were arranged for catechumens, to be read starting from Monday of the third week of the fast. On Wednesday of that same week, the prayers of exorcism were commenced, in preparation for baptism. Similar rites have been observed in Antioch and Spain.[13] These rites of exorcism seem to have been conducted daily, at least in certain places, based on the testimony *The Apostolic Tradition*, "Then from the

---

[10] *The Council of Laodicea*, Canon XLV (NPNF-II 14:153)
[11] *Letter XXXIX* (NPNF-II 4:552)
[12] Baumstark, 190
[13] Ibid., 191

time that they are separated from the other catechumens, hands shall be laid upon them daily in exorcism."[14]

In most cases, the bishop himself conducted the final stages of catechetical instruction, though sometimes this was delegated to a well-trained presbyter. We find an example of this in the homilies of Severus of Antioch, which he delivered every year on the eve of the first Sunday of the fast, and which explained the baptismal rituals of his time to the catechumens. A similar example can be found in Spain, which can be gleaned from the testimony of Justinian the bishop of Valencia, who is known in the manuscript tradition as Ildefonsus of Toledo.[15] These catechetical instructions usually included topics of proper conduct in the church, some theological meditations on the main tenets of the faith, and instruction in the sacraments. These instructions took their form more or less after the council of Nicaea in the 4th century, especially with the agreement over the Nicene creed, though it is important to note that the Nicene creed was by no means the first creedal statement of the Church. In fact, the oldest known creed in the Church is the creed of Der Balyzeh papyrus, which was used in baptisms. The text of this creed, according to the oldest manuscripts of the Alexandrian baptismal rite is:

> I believe in God, Father almighty, in your only-begotten Son, our Lord Jesus Christ, in the Holy Spirit, in the Resurrection of the flesh, in the holy catholic Church.[16]

This same creed was mentioned by Origen in his eighth homily on Exodus,[17] as well as by Pope Dionysius the Great (AD 248-265) in his epistle to his namesake, Dionysius of Rome, regarding Novatian the heretic.[18] There were also other creeds used by different churches,

---

[14] Stewart-Sykes, Alistair. *On the Apostolic Tradition*. (Crestwood, NY, 2001), 106
[15] Baumstark, 191
[16] Deiss, 245. However, it is important to note that J.N.D. Kelly as well as F.E. Brightman have concluded that nothing warrants its dating earlier than the 4th century, making it roughly cotemporaneous with the Nicene creed. Cf. John H. Leith, *Creeds of the Churches: A Reader in Christian Doctrine from the Bible to the Present*, (Louisville, KY 1982), 19. (Ed. Note)
[17] This is another instance where Fr Athanasius leaves much to be desired in terms of attribution. (Ed. Note)
[18] Eusebius, *Ecclesiastical History* VII,8 (NPNF-II 1:296). Though Dionysius in his letter refers to Novatian's overturning the confession that precedes baptism, there is

such as the Roman creed, and the creed of Jerusalem recorded by Cyril of Jerusalem. Of course, it would not have been expected that the Church remained for four centuries without a creed, or a formula for confession of the faith.

We see the Church's seriousness about the handing down of the creed in that the bishop himself used to do so. In an epistle to his sister Marcellina, Ambrose of Milan relates the following, "The day after, which was Sunday, after the lessons and the sermon, when the Catechumens were dismissed, I was teaching the creed to certain candidates in the baptistery of the basilica."[19] Perhaps related to that, we find a reference from Ambrose stating, "Our custom is, for the space of forty days, to deliver public lectures to those who are to be baptized on the doctrine of the Holy and adorable Trinity."[20] The catechumens in turn had to recite the creed in the presence of the bishop or the presbyters on Great Thursday.[21] For this reason, no more names were accepted into the catechumenate after the second week of Lent, as mentioned above.

After instruction in the creed, the catechumens were taught the meaning of the Lord's Prayer. In these final stages, instructors also taught them other short prayers. According to the testimony of Jerome, the Church postponed instruction in the creed and the Lord's Prayer to the end of catechetical instruction and the beginning of the forty day fast, which began a period of revealing the mysteries of their instruction.[22] However, during Holy Week, the Church's entire focus turned to meditating on the suffering of Christ, and his salvific death. Naturally, the catechumens' attention was turned in the same direction, meditating further on the baptism they were about to receive, partaking through it in Christ's death.

Nonetheless, it was understood that this pre-baptismal instruction merely prepares the catechumen to become, in the words of the Council of Nicaea, a novice, and that "For the catechumen himself there is need of time and of a longer trial after baptism," referring to

---

no reason to believe this to be the exact baptismal formula used in Alexandria (Ed. Note)

[19] *Epistle XX*, 4 (NPNF-II 10:423)
[20] To Pammachius against John of Jerusalem, 13 (NPNF-II 6:431)
[21] *Synod of Laodicea,* Canon XLVI (NPNF-II 14:154); *The Council of Trullo,* Canon LXXVIII (NPNF-II 14:399).
[22] To Pammachius Against John of Jerusalem. 13 (NPNF-II 6:431)

those who were elevated to the presbyterate or the episcopate soon after their baptism.[23]

The rudiments of such a lengthy preparation for baptism, which sometimes took two or three years, can still be seen in the modern baptismal rites in many churches, after infant baptism has become the norm. For example, we can see from the *Litany of the Catechumens*, which forms an integral part of the Alexandrian rite, that it could not have been a prayer that was said immediately before baptism, but more likely prayed during the period of catechism, specifically following the weekly sermon. The prayer contains the following entreaty, "Let us ask God the Pantocrator…your servants the catechumens of your people have mercy on them…Grant them that they may know the certainty of the words with which they have been instructed. At the appointed time, may they be worthy of the washing of the new birth, unto forgiveness of their sins."[24]

Concerning the baptism of adults, much can be said also from the church of Armenia. Scholars of liturgy agree that adult baptism persisted in Armenia much longer than any other church, which is taken as evidence for the unique antiquity of the Armenian baptismal rite. As for the reason, the liturgical scholar Frederick Conybeare was of the view that it had to do with the widespread beliefs and practices of the Paulicians in regions around Armenia. Followers of this sect considered valid only those baptisms that were performed on adults, though later by the 8th century, infant baptism had already begun to spread in Armenia as well.[25]

---

[23] *The Council of Nicaea*, Canon II (NPNF-II 14:10). Cf. Canon 80 of The Canons of the Apostles, Canon 10 of the Council of Sardica, and Canon 3 of the Council of Laodicea. Socrates observes that, contrary to the Nicene rule against admitting novices to holy orders, the bishops of Alexandria were in the habit of promoting novices to the offices of readers and singers (*The Council of Trullo*, Canon III NPNF-II 14:363).
[24] Coptic Orthodox Diocese of the Southern United States, *The Holy Baptism* (Colleyville, TX: 2010), 54-55
[25] DACL, 295

5

Infant Baptism

Though the Church prescribed the condition of faith for adult baptism, this is in no way contradicted when infants, the children of baptized Christians, are baptized. That is because the parents of those infants have already declared their faith in Christ, and are seeking to give their children the fruit of that faith, which they have already declared. Perhaps infant baptism would truly be an absurdity if the Church baptized any infant, but this is clearly not the case, since the Church first examines the faith of the parents, or the faith of those to whom the infant is entrusted. A similar analogy to this can be seen in the case of circumcision in the Old Testament.

This analogy is first encountered in Paul's epistle to the Colossians. It was known that circumcision was instituted during the days of Abraham for all male children, "He who is eight days old among you shall be circumcised, every male child in your generations." (Gen 17:12). Comparing this circumcision of the flesh to baptism, Paul writes, "In him you were also circumcised with the circumcision made without hands, by putting off the body of the sins of the flesh, by the circumcision of Christ, buried with him in baptism, in which you also were raised with him through faith in the working of God, who raised him from the dead." (Col 2:11-12) Just as circumcision was the seal of the old covenant[1], baptism is that of the new. In this analogy we see that circumcision was given to all the children of Abraham to enter into the covenant of circumcision, though they were still unable to comprehend the meaning of that covenant. In this we see clearly the similarity with infant baptism.

Since baptism, like circumcision, is a seal for those elected by God to membership of his people, it is only given to those whom the Church recognizes as bearing one of the signs of this election. In the case of adults, this sign is their confession of faith, while in the case of infants, it is their holy covenant through their parents. In this latter

---

[1] Cf. Rom 4:11

case, baptism precedes the child's conscious faith, as we find in Paul's first epistle to the Corinthians, "For the unbelieving husband is sanctified by the wife, and the unbelieving wife is sanctified by the husband; otherwise your children would be unclean, but now they are holy." (I Cor 7:14)[2]

Even adults, though required to profess their faith in Christ before their baptism, were never expected to – nor can they – understand the entire faith and all its depths, which they spend the rest of their lives contemplating and living. This is the case with infant baptism, where full understanding of the faith is not a requirement for baptism, since faith itself is one of the fruits of baptism. One must not forget that our growth in knowledge of Christ and the Church cannot take place except through the Holy Spirit, which we receive in the sacrament of Chrismation. Through the Holy Spirit we come to know Christ as Lord and Savior, "no one can say that Jesus is Lord except by the Holy Spirit." (I Cor 12:3), and through Christ we approach the knowledge of the Father, "No one comes to the Father except through me." (Jn 14:6) This continuous growth is faith in Christ and belief in him, "[We] may grow up in all things into him who is the head—Christ"(Eph 4:15) and, "that Christ may dwell in your hearts through faith; that you, being rooted and grounded in love, may be able to comprehend with all the saints what is the width and length and depth and height, to know the love of Christ which passes knowledge; that you may be filled with all the fullness of God."(Eph 3:17-19). Indeed, this growth in knowledge and love of Christ takes an entire lifetime. It is also faith in the Church through life in her, a faith nourished by the sacraments, the source of the Church's power, and the content of her faith.

While the New Testament did not specifically mention the baptism of infants, it seems to have been a widespread practice in apostolic times. On more than one occasion of baptism, it was mentioned that entire families were baptized, such as the house of Cornelius,[3] the house of Lydia,[4] the keeper of the prison at Philippi,[5] the house

---

[2] John Heron, "Christian Initiation,"*Studia Liturgica* 1(1962): 31-46.
[3] Cf. Acts 10:48
[4] Cf. Acts 16:15
[5] Cf. Acts 16:33

of Crispus,[6] and the house of Stephanas,[7] all of whom likely contained children in addition to adults. In fact, the very promise of forgiveness of sins and receiving the gift of the Holy Spirit was made to the believers and their children, as we find Peter saying, "Repent and be baptized, every one of you, in the name of Jesus Christ for the forgiveness of your sins. And you will receive the gift of the Holy Spirit. The promise is for you and your children and for all who are far off —for all whom the Lord our God will call."(Acts 2:38-39)

Further evidence for infant baptism can be seen in some of the writings of the Fathers. Justin Martyr, in his *First Apology* written between AD 140-150, writes about Christians who have been disciples of Christ at that time for sixty or seventy years. He writes, "And many, both men and women, who have been Christ's disciples from childhood, remain pure at the age of sixty or seventy years; and I boast that I could produce such from every race of men."[8] This means that many people between AD 70 and AD 90 were baptized in infancy, which puts their baptism very close to the time of the apostles.[9] Likewise, Polycarp (AD 69 – 155) reminds his readers of his 68 yearlong discipleship to Christ.[10] Irenaeus also asserts infant baptism, writing, "For he came to save all through means of himself—all, I say, who through him are born again to God—infants, and children, and boys, and youths, and old men."[11]

Likewise, we have ample evidence from the Church of Alexandria that infant baptism existed in Egypt at a very early date.[12] The scholar Origen, who was born of Christian parents, writes in his commentary on Romans, "The Church received from the apostles to give baptism even to infants."[13] Origen also mentions infant baptism as a well-established custom at his time in his eighth homily on Leviticus.[14] Didymus the Blind also seems to agree with this in his treatise

---

[6] Cf. Acts 18:8
[7] Cf. I Cor 1:16
[8] *First Apology* XV (ANF 1:167)
[9] Heron, 39
[10] The Martyrdom of Polycarp, IX (ANF 1:41)
[11] *Against the Heresies*, II, 22:4 (ANF 1:391)
[12] DACL, 258
[13] Cf. Heron, 38
[14] Origen. "Homily VIII on Leviticus," in *Origen: Homilies on Leviticus 1-16* trans. Gary Wayne Barkley, vol. 83 of The Fathers of the Church (Washington DC, CUA Press, 1990), 158

on the Trinity, "Baptism has made all into brethren, without distinction between those who are young through birth, and those who are old."[15]

Other Fathers also, from different backgrounds, agree on infant baptism. Gregory of Nazianzus writes,

> Have you an infant child? Do not let sin get any opportunity, but let him be sanctified from his childhood; from his very tenderest age let him be consecrated by the Spirit. Fearest thou the seal on account of the weakness of nature? O what a small-souled mother, and of how little faith! Why, Anna even before Samuel was born promised him to God, and after his birth consecrated him at once, and brought him up in the priestly habit, not fearing anything in human nature, but trusting in God.[16]

Thus, we see that patristic tradition has maintained since the 3rd century that infants born to Christian parents are granted baptism.[17] Augustine likewise testifies to this, writing, "This the Church always had, always held; this she received from the faith of our ancestors; this she perseveringly guards even to the end."[18] Similar testimonies can be found in many other sources, such as *The Apostolic Constitutions*, Ambrose, John Chrysostom, the writings attributed to Ps.Dionysius, and many others.[19]

On the other hand, the scholar Tertullian opposed infant baptism, advising to postpone their baptism until they are able to know and accept Christ,[20] despite what scripture said, "Let the little children come to me, and do not forbid them; for of such is the kingdom of heaven."(Mt 19:14) By the same token, he preached the postponement of adult baptism for those who were not spiritually mature, since he taught the difficulty or even the impossibility of forgiveness of sins committed after baptism. Such also is the teaching found in

---

[15] *De Trinitate*, PG XXXIX, col. 708
[16] *Oration on Holy Baptism*, XVII (NPNF-II 7:365)
[17] F.L. Cross, The Oxford Dictionary of the Christian Church (ODCC) (London, 1974), 701
[18] *Serm xi De Verb Apost*. This is also an unverified citation from Fr Athanasius (Ed. Note).
[19] Cf. Gerasimos Masarra, *Al-anwar fi Al-asrar*, undated, 49
[20] *On Baptism*, XVIII (ANF 3:677)

the document *The Testament of our Lord* (5th cent.), which enjoyed considerable prominence in the east. This teaching resulted in the widespread custom of postponing baptism, sometimes even close to death, such as the Emperor Constantine himself did.

Nonetheless, today infant baptism is by and large the norm in the Church. As a result, the baptismal texts of the Coptic Church, as well as all the eastern churches, are geared primarily for infant baptisms. This is not the case in all prayers however. For example, the prayer "O master Lord Jesus Christ...heal these children who came to be made catechumens," must be taken metaphorically, since immediately after, it reads "bestow upon them remission of their sins, and grant them by your grace that they may be healed from destroying sin,"[21] which shows clearly that the prayer was intended for adults, and modified later to suit children. This is further shown by the text of all the subsequent prayers in the rite that are titled *A prayer on the Catechumens*, which are invariably directed at adults and not children.[22]

The Church came to be so committed to infant baptism in fact, that certain canons proscribe postponement of baptism. In cases when the infant dies before baptism, either because of the parents' negligence, or because they vowed to baptize their child in a specific place or at the hands of a specific priest, the ecclesiastical canons prescribe fasting, and prohibition from partaking of the holy mysteries for an entire year.[23] Similarly, the canons of Cyril III Ibn Laqlaq (AD 1235-1243) state, "He for whom baptism is possible today, let him not delay it till the morrow on account of the absence of a father or a friend or a garment or an important priest or an affair of rejoicing, for he who delays it without an absolute necessity, God will judge him."[24] In another instance it states, "That customs established in Coptic churches shall not be changed, such as circumcision before baptism, unless prevented by necessity."[25]

The corpus of canons of the Coptic Church contains many other canons pertaining to infant baptism, few of which will be mentioned here. Canon 24 of the canons of Pope Christodoulos (AD 1047-1077)

---

[21] The Holy Baptism, 138
[22] Burmester, O.H.E., "Baptismal Rite of the Coptic Church," *Bulletin de la Societe Archeologie Copte* XI (1945): 62
[23] It is unclear exactly which canons are being referenced here. (Ed. Note)
[24] Burmester, O.H.E., "The Canons of Cyril III Ibn Laklak, 75th Patriarch of Alexandria. Part I" *Bulletin de la Societe Archeologie Copte* XII (1946): 112
[25] Ibid., 107

Infant Baptism

states, "If a presbyter baptizes a child, let the child fast until they are brought forward [to be baptized,][26] and if the child drank his mother's milk, or that of any other of the faithful, they are forbidden from the *qurban* [i.e. the Eucharist], and there is no baptism without *qurban*."[27] Likewise, Abu al-Barakat (ca. AD 1324) gathered some of these canons pertaining to baptisms and stated,

> If an infant is baptized, he is not allowed to drink his mother's milk or anything else until after he partakes of the *qurban*. For if he drank his mother's milk, he is not allowed the *qurban*, and he should not be baptized without *qurban*, therefore, beware of this. And if the baptized was a suckling infant, the service of the mysteries [i.e. the Eucharist] must be started at the same time as the baptismal service, so that they end at the same time, and the infant is baptized and given communion before drinking his mother's milk. Also, be careful in the circumcision of your children, and let no one be baptized except those who have been circumcised, for there is no circumcision after baptism.[28]

Following baptisms, in the Eastern churches, the holy sacraments of chrismation and the Eucharist are administered, as we see clearly in the medieval canons of the Coptic Church, even after infant baptism became the norm. However, in the West, the sacraments of chrismation and the Eucharist came to be postponed until the person is more mature. This change occurred since the time of Augustine, who considered it inappropriate for children to approach the Lord's table, since they are not yet able to examine themselves.[29]

This Western teaching shows a great deal of confusion and contradiction. On the one hand, a person is barred from the Eucharist because they are too young to self-examine, while at the same time they are allowed baptism, while still in the same immature state! The truth is that self-examination before approaching the sacraments is

---

[26] *Vat. Arabe 150* (14th c.) adds, "If the child is able"(Burmester 1945).
[27] Translated from the text as provided by Fr Athanasius.
[28] *Paris Arab. 203* (14th c.) in the Bibliothèque Nationale de Paris, which is *Misbah Al-dhulma fe idah al-khidma* by Abu al-Barakat, chapter 15.
[29] (I Cor 11:28). Cf. Heron, 44

clearly for adults, who are old enough to distinguish between good and evil. Not that this self-examination will determine if a person is actually worthy of the sacrament, but, on the contrary, it will determine how much this person needs the sacrament, a vast difference indeed. As for innocent children, who are still unable to enter into this self-examination, the Lord himself has commanded, "Let the little children come to me, and do not forbid them; for of such is the kingdom of heaven."(Mt 19:14) One must wonder, if these children are not allowed to approach Christ in his holy body and blood, how are they expected to approach him otherwise? Interestingly, Augustine himself wrote, "We believe and affirm the piety and correctness that the faith of the parents and guardians benefits the children, and on this faith they are baptized."[30]

In 1969, the Roman Catholic Church laid down some restrictions on the baptism of infants, if the parents were Christian in name only, which would put the Christian upbringing of the child at risk. In this case, the baptism of the child is postponed until the parents have received an adequate Catholic catechism. Interestingly, these new restrictions were met with opposition by some Western theologians.[31]

On Sponsors

The topic of infant baptism would be incomplete without a brief mention of the office and role of sponsors or what is known currently as *Ishbin*. The word *Ishbin* means a custodian or guard, whereas in Greek the word is 'αναδεχόμενος, which means a guarantor.[32] The sponsor's role is to testify for the person they have sponsored that they are worthy of baptism. In the *Apostolic Tradition* we read,

> When those who are to receive baptism are chosen their lives should be examined; whether they lived uprightly as catechumens, whether they honored the widows, whether they visited the sick, whether they were thorough in performing good works; and if

---

[30] Augustine, *Letter 193:3*. An unverified citation (Ed. Note)
[31] ODCC, 702
[32] Thomas Finn, The Liturgy of Baptism in the Baptismal Instructions of St. John Chrysostom (Washington DC, 1967), 56. Cf. Alexander Schmemann, Of Water and the Spirit. (Crestwood, NY: 1995).

> those who brought them bear witness that they have acted thus, so they should hear the Gospel.[33]

This shows that a sponsor was indeed necessary for adults as well as for children. For adults, a sponsor held the position of a religious instructor of sorts, the spiritual father of the candidate, who guides him in the spiritual path after baptism. However, the sponsor does not speak on behalf of the candidate during the baptismal liturgy itself, which is confirmed by the testimony of Ps. Dionysius the Areopagite in *The Ecclesiastical Hierarchy*.[34]

As for infant baptisms, the sponsor is responsible to raise their child in baptism. The sponsor does not interfere or participate in the rites of baptism, except to speak for the child, who is prevented by age from understanding and responding during the rites of renouncing Satan and professing the faith. In terms of assisting the priest in the baptismal rite, and especially at the moment of submersion, this is rather the duty of the deacons. There is also a mention of deaconesses assisting in this in *The Testament of Our Lord*, a Syriac document describing the baptismal liturgy in the church of Syria.[35]

The custom was for the name of the sponsor to be written along with the candidate's name in the church's records, highlighting the sponsor's spiritual responsibility. In fact, so strong was the connection between the sponsor and the candidate, that the canons of Justinian (AD 483-565) forbade marriage between sponsors and candidates. In addition, church tradition encourages that the sponsors be the parents of the child if they are suitable and fit for this role. Otherwise, a sponsor of the same gender is recommended, someone who is mature, attested to be wise and prudent, knowledgeable of the faith and the mysteries, a pious and virtuous Christian.[36]

This is confirmed by Egyptian tradition, which necessitates that the sponsor be one of the parents or a member of the family, as we find in *The Apostolic Tradition*:

---

[33] Stewart-Sykes, Alistair. *On the Apostolic Tradition.* 20:1,2(Crestwood, NY, 2001), 105-106

[34] The Ecclesiastical Hierarchy II.2.5 In Pseudo-Dionysius: The Complete Works (NY, 1987), 202.

[35] DACL 269

[36] It is unclear here whether Fr Athanasius is paraphrasing the text of a specific canon, or simply describing what is considered the appropriate norms of choosing a baptismal sponsor (Ed. Note).

> You are to baptize the little ones first. All those who are able to speak for themselves should speak. With regard to those who cannot speak for themselves, their parents, or somebody who belongs to their family, should speak.[37]

This is because only the sponsor is allowed to answer for the infant, for whom he is responsible before God. Likewise, Canon 105 of the *Canons of Basil*, which are thought to be of Egyptian provenance, specifies the father, mother, or brother as possible sponsors for the infant. Further advice for sponsors can be found in the baptismal instructions of John Chrysostom, where he writes,

> Do you wish me to address a word to those who are sponsoring you, that they too may know what recompense they deserve if they have shown great care for you, and what condemnation follows if they are careless? Consider, beloved, how those who go surety for someone in a matter of money set up for themselves a greater risk than the one who borrows the money and is liable for it. If the borrower be well disposed, he lightens the burden for his surety; if the dispositions of his soul be ill, he makes the risk a steeper one. Wherefore, the wise man counsels us, saying: 'If thou be surety, think as if thou wert to pay it.'(Sir 8:13) If, then, those who go surety for others in a matter of money make themselves liable for the whole sum, those who go surety for others in matters of the spirit and on an account which involves virtue should be much more alert. They ought to show their paternal love by encouraging, counseling, and correcting those for whom they go surety.
>
> Let them not think that what takes place is a trifling thing, but let them see clearly that they share in the credit if by their admonition they lead those entrusted to them to the path of virtue. Again, if those they sponsor become careless, the sponsors themselves will suffer great punishment. That is why it is

---

[37] Stewart-Sykes, 21:4. 110

customary to call the sponsors 'spiritual fathers' that they may learn by this very action how great an affection they must show to those they sponsor in the matter of spiritual instruction. If it is a noble thing to lead to a zeal for virtue those who are in no way related to us, much more should we fulfill this precept in the case of the one whom we receive as a spiritual son.[38]

Theodore of Mopsuestia also writes the following regarding sponsors:

> As regards you…who come to baptism, a duly appointed person inscribes your name in the church book, together with that of your godfather, who answers for you and becomes your guide in the city and the leader of your citizenship therein. This is done in order that you may know that you are, long before the time and while still on earth, enrolled in heaven, and that your godfather who is in it has the great diligence necessary to teach you, who are a stranger and a newcomer to that great city, all the things that pertain to it and to its citizenship, so that you should be conversant with its life without any trouble and anxiety.[39]

Along the same line, we provide here from the Coptic baptismal rite the full text of the commandment for the sponsors, which says,

> Blessed brethren, understand the amount of dignity, which your children have obtained, who have been counted among the chosen, and the grace with which they have been dyed. They have now been counted among the Christians, by the pure baptism that was commanded by the savior of the world, as witnessed by the chosen, pure apostles. That after the holy Resurrection, he appeared to them and sent them to all nations to preach to them, saying, 'Go

---

[38] The Second Baptismal Instruction II, 15. (ACW 31), 48-49
[39] Finn, 55

therefore and make disciples of all the nations, baptizing them in the name of the Father and of the Son and of the Holy Spirit, teaching them to observe all things that I have commanded you; and lo, I am with you always, even to the end of the age.' (Mt 28:19-20)

Today, my beloved, your children have become inheritors of life with Jesus Christ. Today, your children have received a bond of life, and have become rooted in the true Orthodox faith. The day on which they were born, they were slaves and not free. But today, they have become conquerors of the plots of the wicked.

Did you hear the fearful words that were told you about the holy baptism? Did you not answer on behalf of your children, saying, 'We renounce you, Satan, and all your unclean works?' Did you not accept them toward the east and submitted to the Lord, saying, 'We believe in one God, God the Father the Pantocrator, and his only-begotten Son, Jesus Christ our Lord, and the holy, life-giving Spirit?' And confessed the one baptism in the holy Church, hearkening to his divine saying in the Holy Gospel by the tongues of his pure saintly apostles, 'Unless one is born of water and the Spirit, he cannot enter the kingdom of God" (Jn 3:5)?

Now, my beloved, understand that you have received your children by the holy, pure, spiritual baptism, and that he will require it of you if you neglect them and their discipline and their restoration from unacceptable circumstances.

Work diligently in teaching them to read the holy scriptures which are the breath of God, and in attending the church in matins and vespers, and fasting on Wednesdays and Fridays, the holy forty days, and all the fasts and in keeping the Church laws and apostolic commands. They now have become worthy to partake of the holy mysteries of God, which are the body and blood of the Son of God, which was shed for the salvation of the creation.

Safeguard your children, and preserve them from going to unsuitable places, so that the Lord may guard them from satanic temptations. Sow in them beautiful qualities. Sow in them righteousness and praise. Sow in them purity. Sow in them obedience and love and holiness. Sow in them compassion, charity and justice. Sow in them piety, patience and righteousness. Sow in them honesty and all the good works that please God that your souls and your children's may live.

And you, blessed godparents and pious trustees and brethren, may God protect you with his mighty right hand. May he become a protector to you as he was with our father Abraham. Know that you have been called as sponsors for this baptism, and, from today, you are their spiritual parents, observers of their secrets, responsible for their wrongdoings, and observers of their daily circumstances. Today you are accountable for their actions and deeds, and have become guarantors from Christ to the true assurance, that you may answer on their behalf on judgment day.

You assumed this talent under the law, and the priests of God and the Church have required of you to be diligent in teaching them good conduct and purity, that you may experience utmost pride in them. Teach them the ways of God so that their ways may be acceptable, satisfactory and illuminated. Build them upon the foundation of righteousness. Avert them from interacting with the worldly, the lecherous, evildoers and the wicked and partaking in their entertainment, amusement, and mockery.

Nurture them with spiritual teachings. Teach them the fear of God and his commandments. Raise them according to an economy and sound order. Do not neglect their catechism like the wicked and lazy servant who neglected his talent, but be diligent that you may hear his voice saying, 'Well done, good and faithful servant; you were faithful over a few things, I will make you ruler over many things.' (Mt 25:23)

May God make you, brethren who hearken, successful in your talents, through the grace of our Lord and Savior, Jesus Christ, whom we ask to make us steadfast in the Orthodox faith to the last breath, to forgive us our sins and iniquities, to cover our oversights, help us to do what is pleasing to him, and to crush Satan underneath our feet speedily. May he make the gates of the church open in our faces, and make us hear his voice full of joy saying, 'Come to me, you blessed of my Father, inherit the kingdom prepared for you from the foundation of the world. Through the intercession of our lady of us all, Virgin Mary, and all those who have pleased the Lord with their good deeds since Adam to the end of the ages, Amen.[40]

Unfortunately, the role of the sponsor today has become a mere formality. In most cases, the mother fulfills this role, even if she is ignorant of the Church and the faith, and does not fulfill the canonical requirements for selecting a sponsor. In fact, her role is restricted to the liturgical service of baptism, with the result being that many children, though born to Christian parents and baptized in the Church, do not grow up to be particularly involved in or committed to the Church. Statistics estimate that only 20% of baptized Coptic Christians are frequent goers to Church services.[41]

Indeed, the enormous efforts of countless servants and shepherds to attract the souls of those who are not unbelievers but Christians in name only could have been saved if only children were raised under the guidance of pious and meticulous sponsors. The first five years of a child's life are the most dangerous, and form the foundation

---

[40] The Holy Baptism, 181-185
[41] Unfortunately, Fr Athanasius does not provide any source for this statistic. In the absence of any official census or studies conducted by the Church, it is difficult to understand how he could have arrived at this number (Ed. Note).

of the rest of the child's life. Let's not pretend that Sunday school, to which our children are brought at the age of five or six, and last for an hour or two every week, is capable on its own to direct the child's spiritual formation in a deep way. On the contrary, it is only the home that can do so, and with proper and careful supervision. This is the enormity of the real burden on the shoulders of every mother that takes it upon herself to become a sponsor for her child. How will such a mother respond, if she does not raise her child in the fear of God and love of the Church? At the same time, we cannot ignore the many cases in which the Church fails to take the suitability of the mother as a sponsor into consideration before baptism. This matter is indeed of grave importance, for the mothers of today are raising the Church of tomorrow.

6

The Absolution of Women

The absolution of women is a rite the Church performs on women forty days after giving birth to a male infant, or eighty days after giving birth to a female infant. The question that is raised by many is, when did this practice start, and what is the liturgical history of this practice in the Eastern churches in general?

The Jews, according to their laws, were the first to go to great lengths in their practices regarding things considered clean, and others deemed unclean, especially as these laws pertained to entering the temple, participating in Passover, eating of the holy bread, and any other religious observance. Only those deemed pure were permitted to approach the temple of Yahweh.[1] In particular, chapter twelve of the book of Leviticus examines in detail the purity laws of the Old Testament. On the other hand, the New Testament clearly states, "What God has cleansed you must not call common," (Acts 10:15) and that uncleanness abides in sin alone, which separates us from God. All the observances required by the laws of purity according to the Levitical priesthood, or the priesthood of Aaron, things that were considered unclean according to the old law, were abrogated by the new covenant, which was established upon the priesthood of Christ himself, according to the order of Melchizedek and not Aaron, as the epistle to the Hebrews states, "the priesthood being changed, of necessity there is also a change of the law." (Heb 7:12) Nonetheless, the issue of purity remained a hot issue for the Church of the new covenant, insofar as the Church found herself still in a Jewish milieu, which made it difficult to completely get rid of the restrictions of the old law, despite what St Paul wrote in his epistles to raise the minds of his readers from the law of the old covenant, to the grace of the new.

---

[1] Cf. Lev 7:19-21; 22:3; Num 9:6; 18:11; 1 Sam 21:5

Infant Baptism

Christ himself obeyed the laws of purity in order to unbind the children of the new covenant from the ancient ordinances, which he fulfilled in order to lift them up from upon our shoulders, and thus Christ came "to fulfill all righteousness." (Mt 3:15) Likewise, St Mary herself obeyed these laws, and was considered unclean according to the law for seven days after giving birth to the divine child, though she is the pure and ever-virgin saint. Afterwards, she remained thirty-three days in the blood of her purification,[2] though she is the one that gave birth to God the Word, while her virginity remained sealed! Thus, through Mary the second Eve, the sin of the first Eve was blotted out. Through the first Eve came the curse, and through the second, salvation from the judgment of the law and its ancient ordinances.

In this chapter, I will discuss two main points that cover the topic of the absolution of women both historically and theologically. First, I will provide an overview of the Church's position regarding natural bodily secretions, and the period of purification for menstruating and postpartum women. Second, I will discuss the difference in the period of time required for purification in the case of giving birth to a male or a female child.

The Church's Position Regarding Natural Secretions

The ancient Coptic tradition has always maintained that the natural bodily secretions of both men and women should not prevent the person from praying, reading the Scriptures, and attending church, but only forbid them from partaking of the Eucharist, particularly during a woman's menstrual cycle and after giving birth. This tradition has been followed throughout the centuries, supported by the writings and sayings of the fathers of the Coptic Church specifically. This is so, not because these natural occurrences are considered unclean, since after baptism there no longer remains any uncleanness, except that of sin. This is the understanding that prevailed in the Church of Alexandria from the beginning. In the *Apostolic Tradition* of Hippolytus, which spread in the Church of Egypt since the 3rd century under the title of *The Egyptian Church Order*, we find the following statement: "Let them teach those appointed for baptism that they

---

[2] Cf. Lev 12:4

should wash and be made free; that they should be made such on the fifth Sabbath. And if there is a woman who is after the custom of women, let her be put apart, and let her receive baptism another day."[3] In another place, the text also states, "But thou who art bound in marriage, refrain not from prayer, for you are not defiled. For those who have washed have no need to wash again, for they are purified and are clean."[4]

This is the same tradition referred to by Pope Dionysius the Great of Alexandria (AD 248-265) in his epistle to Basilides the Bishop of Pentapolis, where he writes:

> The question touching women in the time of their separation, whether it is proper for them when in such a condition to enter the house of God, I consider a superfluous inquiry. For I do not think that, if they are believing and pious women, they will themselves be rash enough in such a condition either to approach the holy table or to touch the body and blood of the Lord. Certainly the woman who had the issue of blood of twelve years' standing did not touch the Lord himself, but only the hem of his garment, with a view to her cure. (Mt 9:20; Lk 8:43) For to pray, however a person may be situated, and to remember the Lord, in whatever condition a person may be, and to offer up petitions for the obtaining of help, are exercises altogether blameless. But the individual, who is not perfectly pure both in soul and in body, shall be interdicted from approaching the holy of holies.[5]

Likewise, he writes in the same epistle:

> As to those who are overtaken by an involuntary flux in the night-time, let such follow the testimony of their own conscience, and consider themselves as to whether they are doubtfully minded in this matter or not. And he that doubteth in the matter of meats,

---

[3] Tattam, 52
[4] Ibid., 86
[5] The Works of Dionysius: Extant Fragments. (ANF 6:96)

the apostle tells us, 'is damned if he eat.' (Rom 15:23) In these things, therefore, let everyone who approaches God be of a good conscience, and of a proper confidence, so far as his own judgment is concerned.[6]

This Egyptian tradition can be seen also at the time of Athanasius the Great, when he writes to Amun, one of the desert fathers of Nitria,

> All things made by God are beautiful and pure, for the Word of God has made nothing useless or impure. For 'we are a sweet savor of Christ in them that are being saved,' (II Cor 2:15) as the apostle says. But since the devil's darts are varied and subtle, and he contrives to trouble those who are of simpler mind, and tries to hinder the ordinary exercises of the brethren, scattering secretly among them thoughts of uncleanness and defilement; come let us briefly dispel the error of the evil one by the grace of the Savior, and confirm the mind of the simple.
>
> For tell me, beloved and most pious friend, what sin or uncleanness there is in any natural secretion,—as though a man were minded to make a culpable matter of the cleanings of the nose or the sputa from the mouth? And we may add also the secretions of the belly, such as are a physical necessity of animal life. Moreover if we believe man to be, as the divine Scriptures say, a work of God's hands, how could any defiled work proceed from a pure power? And if, according to the divine Acts of the Apostles, 'we are God's offspring,' (Acts 17:28) we have nothing unclean in ourselves. For then only do we incur defilement, when we commit sin, that foulest of things. But when any bodily excretion takes place independently of will, then we experience this, like other things, by a necessity of nature.

---

[6] Ibid.

He is blessed who, being freely yoked in his youth, naturally begets children. But if he uses nature licentiously, the punishment of which the Apostle writes shall await whoremongers and adulterers.[7]

So then their unclean and evil objections had their proper solution long since given in the divine Scriptures.[8]

Likewise, Pope Timothy I (AD 380-385) follows the same tradition. In the *Canonical Responses* attributed to him, we read:

Question 5: If a woman lies with her husband at night, or a man with his wife, and they have intercourse, should they take communion, or not?

Answer: They ought not. For the apostle proclaimed, 'Do not deprive one another except with consent for a time, that you may give yourselves to fasting and prayer; and come together again so that Satan does not tempt you because of your lack of self-control.' (I Cor 7:5)

Question 6: If a female catechumen has given her name in order to be baptized [lit. enlightened], and on the day of baptism, occurs to her according to the custom of women. Ought she to be baptized in that day, or postponed, and how long?

Answer: She ought to wait, until she is purified.

Question 7: If a woman is found to be in the period according to the custom of women, ought she to approach the mysteries on that day, or not?

Answer: She ought not, until she is purified.[9]

---

[7] Cf. Heb 13:14
[8] Letter XLVIII: Letter to Amun. (NPNF-II 4:556)
[9] PG XXXIII, 1300. While Fr Athanasius uses the Arabic translation for these canons found in Archimandrite Hananiah Kassab, *Majmu'at Al-Shar' Al-kanasy*, (Manshurat Al-nur, 1975), 909, the translation here is from the original Greek text, which at times is more verbose than Kassab's Arabic. (Ed. Note)

From the 6th century, we find the canons of Hippolytus addressing the same issue. These canons were originally written in Greek in the 6th century, and later translated to Arabic, providing us with our only extant version.[10] In these canons we read,

> If there is a woman who is after the custom of women, she is not to be baptized at that time, but she is to be delayed until she is purified.[11]

And again,

> He who is bound in marriage, though he may rise up from near his wife, let him pray. For marriage is undefiled, and he does not need to bathe with water after the second birth, apart from washing his hands only. For the Holy Spirit anoints the body of the believer, and purifies it completely.[12]

In addition, the Church's position in the 10th century can be found in the writings of Sawirus ibn Al-Muqaffa', the bishop of El Ashmunein (Hermopolis). He writes,

> When Adam and Eve obeyed the devil and listened to him, the power of God abandoned them, and there was aroused in them the desire for mingling at this hour...For this reason, their descendants were commanded to fast from this desire at a certain time, as the second book of the Torah says that when God wanted to descend on the mountain to address the children of Israel, he told Moses, command them not to come near their wives for three days and to be purified, then I will descend and speak to you in their presence.[13] Likewise, the Torah says in the

---

[10] In the introduction to his work on the canons of Hippolytus, Coquin asserts that we no longer possess any fragments from the Coptic or Greek text of these canons. Nonetheless, he maintains that they are translated from an original Sahidic Coptic text currently lost, which was in turn translated from a Greek original. He bases these assertions on analyzing some of the words and phrases found in the Arabic translation. Cf. R.G. Coquin, *Les Canons D'Hippolyte*, PO 31 (Paris, 1966), 277.
[11] Canon 19:5
[12] Canon 27:3
[13] Cf. Ex 19

book of the law, if a man lies with his wife, he must bathe with water, and remains unclean until the evening of that day. And if he does not bathe, he shall remain unclean for seven days.[14]

This command was issued by God to show us that this desire has entered us since the transgression [i.e. the fall], and that it defiles us when it is expelled from us, and that it is our duty to fast as much as we are able, because it is in our nature. So when our Lord Jesus Christ came and loosened us from the bonds of the law and the Torah, and bound us instead with his yoke that is sweet and light, he did not command us to abstain from our wives for three days before we hear his words, as the children of Israel did. Nor did he declare us defiled because of lying with our wives, nor did he prevent us from her and from lying with her, nor did he stipulate bathing in water because of lying with her, or because of intercourse. Nor did he prohibit us from prayer, or entering the church as he did with the children of Israel. Instead, he lightened his yoke upon us, and made his law easier so that we may be able to bear it, and he said, it is not a defilement, but rather a breaking of fast. He who breaks his fast ought not to abstain from praying, or from entering the church, or attending the liturgy, but only from partaking of the bread...

Intercourse does not defile after baptism, neither does lying with one's lawful wife, but it is merely a breaking of the fast, and he who breaks his fast is not defiled, and has not sinned in his breaking his fast, unless he broke it on a day of fast. For he who breaks his fast during a fast sins just as Adam sinned by eating when he was prohibited from doing so. Thus, Paul commands both man and woman not to

---

[14] Sawirus grossly misinterprets the text of Leviticus referenced here (Lev 15:16-18), confusing men with an emission of semen, with those who have intercourse with their wives (Ed. Note).

Infant Baptism

> abstain from one another except through mutual agreement during the days of the fast. And this does not prevent them form praying, or attending liturgy, but only from partaking of the bread...[15]
>
> Neither does he mention bathing at all, for intercourse with one's lawful wife is not a defilement. And if it were a defilement, indeed water does not purify the defiled, but only washes the filth of the flesh. But lawful intercourse is not defiling, but rather fornication is defiling. A fornicator cannot be purified, even if he washed in the waters of all the seas and rivers, but he is purified when he regrets and repents of his fornication. Likewise, the rule regarding nocturnal emissions is the same as the one for lying with one's wife.[16]

This is the tradition of the Coptic Church for the first one thousand years, verified and supported by the witness of the Fathers. However, as far as the purification of a woman after giving birth – though it is a state that does not differ from the previous cases regarding marital relations – we find here an opinion from Origen that is peculiar to him, and one that sets him apart from the rest of tradition. In his commentary on chapter twelve of the book of Leviticus, he comments on the verse, "Then the Lord spoke to Moses, saying, 'Speak to the children of Israel, saying: 'If a woman has conceived, and borne a male child, then she shall be unclean seven days; as in the days of her customary impurity she shall be unclean. And on the eighth day the flesh of his foreskin shall be circumcised. She shall then continue in the blood of her purification thirty-three days. She shall not touch any hallowed thing, nor come into the sanctuary until the days of her purification are fulfilled'," (Lev 12:1-4) he writes,

> For the lawgiver added this word to distinguish her who conceived and gave birth without seed from other women so as not to designate as unclean every

---

[15] Cf. I Cor 7:5. Sawirus seems again to imply that Scripture commands something that it clearly does not. In the passage cited from Paul's letter to the Corinthians, there is no mention of whether those who are married should or should not partake of the Eucharist after intercourse. (Ed. Note)

[16] Sawirus ibn Al-Muqaffa', *Al-dorr Al-thamin fi Idah Al-din*, (Cairo, undated), 149-154.

woman who had given birth but her who had given birth by receiving seed. There can also be added to this the fact that this law, which is written concerning uncleanness pertains to women. But concerning Mary, it is said that a virgin conceived and gave birth. Therefore, let women carry the burdens of the law, but let virgins be immune from them...

Now therefore, let us also inquire what may be the reason that a woman, who in this world furnishes a service for those who are born, is said to become unclean not only when she received the seed, but also when she gave birth. From this also she is commanded to offer 'the young pigeons or turtledoves for sin at the door of the tent of witness' (Lev 12:6) for her purification that the priest may make propitiation for her as if she owes a propitiation and a purification for sin because she furnishes the service of bearing a man into this world. For so it is written, 'And the priest will intercede for her and she will be clean.' (Lev 12:7) I myself in such matters dare to say nothing. Yet, I think there are some hidden mysteries contained in these things and there is some hidden secret, for which the woman who conceives by the seed and gives birth is called unclean, just as the one guilty of sin is commanded to offer a sacrifice for sin and thus to be purified.

But Scripture also declares that one himself who is born whether male or female is not 'clean from filth although his life is one day.' (Job 14:4-5) And that you may know that there is something great in this and such that it has not come from the thought of any of the saints; not one from all the saints is found to have celebrated a festive day or a great feast on the day of his birth. No one is found to have had joy on the day of the birth of his son or daughter...

But if it pleases you to hear what other saints also might think about this birthday, hear David speaking, 'In iniquity I was conceived and in sins my mother brought me forth,' (Ps 50:7) showing that every soul which is born in flesh is polluted by the filth of iniquity and sin; and for this reason we can say what we already have recalled above, 'No one is pure from uncleanness even if his life is only one day long.' (Job 14:4-5)[17]

From this we can see Origen's private opinion, which differs from the general opinion of the fathers of the Church of Alexandria. As far as the ancient Syriac tradition, indeed it agrees with the Coptic tradition on this matter except in allowing women during their period of purification to partake of the holy mysteries. This is indicated in *The Arabic Didascalia* (the Arabic translation of *The Apostolic Constitutions*), which goes back to the mid-fourth century. In this text, we find,

> Wherefore marriage is honorable and comely, and the begetting of children pure, for there is no evil in that which is good. Therefore neither is the natural purgation abominable before God, who has ordered it to happen to women within the space of thirty days for their advantage and healthful state, who do less move about, and keep usually at home in the house.[18]

> Do not therefore keep any such observances about legal and natural purgations, as thinking you are defiled by them. Neither do you seek after Jewish separations[19]

> Thou therefore, O woman, if, as thou sayest, in the days of thy separation thou art void of the Holy Spirit, thou art then filled with the unclean one; for by neglecting to pray and to read thou wilt invite him to thee, though he were unwilling. For this spirit, of all others, loves the ungrateful.[20]

---

[17] Origen. "Homily VIII on Leviticus," in *Origen: Homilies on Leviticus 1-16* trans. Gary Wayne Barkley, vol. 83 of The Fathers of the Church (Washington DC, CUA Press, 1990), 154-158
[18] *Constitutions of the Holy Apostles,* Book VII, Sec V, xxviii (ANF 7:463)
[19] Ibid., 464
[20] Ibid., 462

> Wherefore, O woman, eschew such vain words, and be ever mindful of God that created thee, and pray to him. For He is thy Lord, and the Lord of the universe; and meditate in his laws without observing any such things, such as the natural purgation, lawful mixture, child-birth, a miscarriage, or a blemish of the body; since such observations are the vain inventions of foolish men, and such inventions as have no sense in them... Wherefore, beloved, avoid and eschew such observations, for they are heathenish.[21]
>
> For if thou thinkest, O woman, when thou art seven days in thy separation, that thou art void of the Holy Spirit, then if thou shouldest die suddenly thou wilt depart void of the Spirit, and without assured hope in God. Or else thou must imagine that the Spirit always is inseparable from thee, as not being in a place. But thou standest in need of prayer and the Eucharist, and the coming of the Holy Ghost. For neither lawful mixture, nor child- bearing, nor the menstrual purgation, nor nocturnal pollution, can defile the nature of a man, or separate the Holy Spirit from him.[22]

In the Syriac version of *The Apostolic Constitutions* in its French translation, we find this alternate text:

> For if you possess the Holy Spirit within you, and you stay away without being forbidden from prayer, the books, or the Eucharist, take heed then and notice that prayer is heard by means of the Holy Spirit, and the Eucharist is accepted and sanctified by the Holy Spirit, and the holy books are the words of the Holy Spirit. Therefore, if the Holy Spirit is in you, why do you guard against approaching the works of the Holy Spirit like those who say, "Whoever swears by the altar, it is nothing; but whoever swears by the

---

[21] Ibid.
[22] Ibid.

gift that is on it, he is obliged to perform it. Fools and blind! For which is greater, the gift or the altar that sanctifies the gift? Therefore he who swears by the altar, swears by it and by all things on it. He who swears by the temple, swears by it and by him who dwells in it. And he who swears by heaven, swears by the throne of God and by him who sits on it." (Mt 23:18-22)

Therefore, if you have the Holy Spirit, yet you refrain from his fruits and do not approach them, hear also our Lord Jesus Christ [say], O you foolish and blind woman, which is greater, the bread or the Holy Spirit that sanctifies the bread? For if you have the Holy Spirit, you are in fact observing vain customs, whereas if you do not have the Holy Spirit, how can you perform works of righteousness? For the Holy Spirit remains always with those who possess him. For if the Holy Spirit departs from someone, the wicked spirit clings to him, for the wicked spirit when it departs from a person, goes and chooses a place without water, that is, people that have not entered the water, and were not baptized.[23]

It is clear therefore from the Syriac tradition that the natural purification of a woman – whether during her menstrual period or after giving birth – does not prevent her from prayer, reading the Bible, attending church, and even partaking of the Eucharist. According to the Syriac tradition, a woman's staying home for thirty days after giving birth is not because of defilement or impurity, but simply for her to regain her health.

---

[23] This passage was translated directly from the Arabic text provided by Fr Athanasius. (Ed. Note)

Epilogue

The mystery of our initiation into the Eucharistic community of the people of God is one of such depth that it was understood in light of various Biblical stories surrounding the central ideas of salvation and birth. It is death and resurrection with Christ, it is birth from the womb that is the Church, and it is also the new crossing of the sea for the people of God, to name a few. Despite the multiplicity of Biblical foundations of baptism, one finds himself in the final analysis before a mystical reality that far exceeds all approximations, types, and symbols. That is because only in the New Covenant can we properly speak of a mystical death and resurrection with Christ, a mystical pascha, of which every Christian partakes, and which – like all the mysteries of the Church – is accomplished through the operation of the Holy Spirit in the new time. This mystery is also fundamentally ecclesial, a liturgy in the proper sense of the word. This ecclesial character cannot be emphasized enough, and takes its full manifestation in the unbroken link between baptism and the Eucharist. Indeed, baptism is after all a form of initiation into the Christian community, a community that is essentially Eucharistic in character.

The purpose of this work was to provide a snapshot of how baptism was understood by the fathers and the early Church. In particular, the Scriptural foundation of baptism was the main focus of Part I, in which Fr Matthew the Poor offered deep meditations on the various types of baptism in the Old Testament, as well as instances of baptism in the New Testament. This Scriptural foundation is indispensable to acquiring the mind of the Church, and beginning to grasp the various angles by which baptism was understood by the fathers. Fr Matthew's presentation and writing style is rich and profound, yet simple, a quality that is unfortunately lacking in many products of academic theology. Here we have the clear and transparent thoughts of an unassuming contemporary saint, concerned first and foremost with reaching the average Christian, in need of a deeper relationship with the holy mysteries of the Church. It is out of the same desire that this translation into English was made, in order to make profound writings about the mysteries of the Church available to the wide audience of the Coptic Orthodox Church in English-speaking countries.

Of no less influence is the selections presented here by Fr Athanasius Al-Maqary. In Part II of this work, the history of the celebration of baptism is explained from various perspectives. Through historical, patristic, and liturgical sources, Fr Athanasius explored how baptism was accomplished in various areas in the early Church, how the catechumenate worked, when baptism was usually conferred, and how infant baptism was the norm throughout the Church's early centuries. The purpose of this investigation into the history of baptism is to show how the Church remained faithful to the Scriptural foundation of the sacrament, and how this played out in the early centuries of Christianity. As is natural with any historical investigation, not all questions can be adequately answered. Sometimes, as a cautious historian, the author may have refrained from making rigid concluding statements, preferring instead to present the historical data without much commentary. Some might be inclined to consider this avoidance of difficult subjects in need of a more honest discussion. However, it is important to keep in mind that the duty of a historian is to inform, and not to reform.

Once again, by providing this accessible English translation of this historical background on baptism, it is my hope to encourage a more informed approach to the sacraments of the Church and her liturgical tradition, which is the critical prerequisite behind any honest and productive discussion about the meaning of our sacramental life in Christ, to him be glory at all times.

Bibliography

Abdallah, A. *L'Ordinamento Liturgico di Gabriele V 88 Patriarcho Copto (1409-27)*. Cairo, 1962.

Annick, Martin. *Athanase d'Alexandrie et l'Eglise d'Egypte au IVe siècle (328-373)*. Rome, 1996.

Atiya, Aziz S., ed. *The Coptic Encyclopedia*. NY: Macmillan, 1991.

Baumstark, Anton. *Comparative Liturgy*. London, 1958.

Burmester, O.H.E. "Baptismal Rite of the Coptic Church." *Bulletin de la Societe Archeologie Copte* XI (1945): 81-136.

_____ , "The Canons of Cyril III Ibn Laklak, 75th Patriarch of Alexandria. Part I" *Bulletin de la Societe Archeologie Copte* XII (1946):

Butler, A.J. *The Ancient Coptic Churches of Egypt*. Vol. 2. Oxford, 1884.

Cabrol, Fernand, and Dom Henri Leclreq. *Dictionnaire d'Archeologie Chretienne et de Liturgie*. Paris, 1925.

Coptic Orthodox Diocese of the Southern United States. *The Holy Baptism*. Colleyville, TX, 2010.

Coquin, R.G. "Les Canons D'Hippolyte." *PO*, 1966.

Cross, F.L. *The Oxford Dictionary of the Christian Church*. London, 1974.

Cyril of Alexandria, Philip Edward Pusey, Henry Parry Liddon, and Thomas Randell. *The Commentary on the Gospel According to St. John*. England: Oriental Orthodox Library, 2006.

Danielou, Jean. *From Shadows to Reality: Studies in the Biblical Typology of the Fathers.* Westminster, MD: The Newman Press, 1960.

Deiss, Lucien. *Springtime of the Liturgy: Liturgical Texts from the First Four Centuries.* Collegeville, MN: The Liturgical Press, 1979.

Evetts, B.T.A. "The History of the Patriarchs of the Coptic Church of Alexandria, Arabic Text Edited, Translated and Annotated." *PO*, 1912.

Finn, Thomas. *The Liturgy of Baptism in the Baptismal Instructions of St. John Chrysostom.* Washington, DC, 1967.

Hamman, A.G. *Baptism: Ancient Liturgies and Patristic Texts.* Staten Island, NY: Alba House, 1967.

Heron, John. "Christian Initiation." *Studia Liturgica*, March 1962: 33-34.

John Chrysostom, and P.W. Harkins. *Baptismal Instructions.* Mahwah, NY: Paulist Press, 1963.

Johnson, Maxwell. *The Christian Rites of Initiation: Their Evolution and Interpretation.* Collegeville, MN: The Liturgical Press, 2007.

Jungmann, Josef A. The Early Liturgy to the Time of Gregory the Great. London: Darton, Longman & Todd, 1959.

Kassab, Hananiah. *Majmu'at Al-shar' Al-kanasy* (The Collection of Ecclesiastical Ruling). Beirut: Manshurat Al-nur, 1975.

Lantchoot, A. van. "Le Ms. Vatic. Copte 44 et le livre de Chreme (MSS. Paris Arabe 100)." *Le Museon*, 1932: 5-6.

Leith, John H. *Creeds of the Churches: A Reader in Christian Doctrine from the Bible to the Present.* Louisville, KY, 1982.

Liddell, Henry George, and Robert Scott. *Greek-English Lexicon.* Oxford: Oxford University Press, 1996.

Masarra, Gerasimos. *Al-anwar fi Al-asrar* (The Lights in the Mysteries), undated.

Origen. *Homilies on Leviticus 1-16*. Washington, DC: Catholic University of America, 1990.

_____, and Ronald Heine. *Homilies on Genesis and Exodus*. Washington DC: Catholic University of America, 1982.

Porphyry, and George Francis Hill. *The Life of Porphyry, Bishop of Gaza*. Oxford: Clarendon Press, 1913.

Pseudo-Dionysius. *The Complete Works*. NY, 1987.

Qelada, William Soliman. *Al-disqolia: Ta'lim Al-rosol* (The Didascalia, The Teaching of the Apostles). Cairo, 1979.

Roberts, Alexander, and James Donaldson. *Ante-Nicene Fathers*. Peabody, MA: Hendrickson Publishers, 1995.

Schaff, Philip, and Henry Wace. *Nicene and Post-Nicene Fathers*. Peabody, MA: Hendrickson Publishers, 1995.

Schmemann, Alexander. *For the Life of the World: Sacraments and Orthodoxy*. Crestwood, NY: St. Vladimir Seminary Press, 1973.

_____. *Of Water and the Spirit: A Liturgical Study of Baptism*. Crestwood, NY: St. Vladimir Seminary Press, 1995.

Sawirus ibn Al-Muqaffa'. *Al-dorr Al-thamin fi Idah Al-din* (The Precious Jewel in the Clarification of the Religion). Cairo.

Stewart-Sykes, Alistair. *On the Apostolic Tradition*. Crestwood, NY: St. Vladimir Seminary Press, 2001.

Tattam, Henry. *The Apostolical Constitutions or The Canons of the Apostles in Coptic with an English Translation*. London, 1848.

Wilkinson, John. *Egeria's Travels*. Oxford, 2006.

www.ingramcontent.com/pod-product-compliance
Lightning Source LLC
Chambersburg PA
CBHW031422290426
44110CB00011B/482